Fly Fishing
Montana's Missouri River

text and photography by *Trapper Badovinac*

Dedication

To Grandpa, who never got mad when I couldn't tell the difference between grass and the newly sprouted blades of corn I was hoeing, and for taking me fishing with equal patience. Thanks for labeling me "The fishinest kid I ever knew."

To Dad, who shared his love of the outdoors with me in many ways and on many lakes and trout streams. And for imparting meaningful wisdom that took me years to appreciate.

And to Mom, for cooking all those critters Dad and I brought home, be they finned, feathered, or furred, but mostly thanks for being so loving, patient, and kind.

FRONT COVER: *The Blue Ribbon section of the Missouri between Holter Dam and the town of Cascade is home to prolific aquatic insect hatches and the trout that grow fat and sassy in this rich environment.*

BACK COVER: *Four seasons on the Missouri.*

ISBN 1-56037-249-4
© 2003 Farcountry Press

Photography © Trapper Badovinac
Illustrations page 81, 83 © Mark Lewis

Table of Contents

The turning leaves signal the end is near for the prolific hatches for this season.

Introduction

Fly fishing. For many, just the words invoke a dream-like mist revealing a solitary angler casting effortlessly to rising trout along a bank—a man with a rod plying his skill against those who live and die by their instincts. The target is spotted, the fly delivered just upstream of the anxiously waiting fish. A slight lateral adjustment by the fish lines him up with his next food morsel and as his mouth opens and pulls in the presented fraud, the angler knows the fish will make the discovery soon enough. As the white mouth closes, the rod lifts, setting the hook. The predator becomes the prey and quickly changes tactics from stalk to escape. The angler's heart rate jumps into passing gear. The extra adrenaline begins to shake his hands and knees, leaving him clumsy with his line and reel. Nothing is going to wipe that crazy grin from his face. This is fly fishing. The universe shrinks to those 30 or 40 feet between the angler and the fish and nothing else exists. The angler's mind is cleared of extraneous thought. There is now no room for the problems of the office, whether the kid will get into the college of his choice, or that mutual fund that isn't doing as well as expected. It's just the angler, the fish, and the water.

Fly fishing the Missouri River in Montana can often make this dream a reality. Much of the river from the headwaters to where it joins the mighty Mississippi offers great fishing for various cold and warm water species, but the 35-mile section from Holter Dam to the town of Cascade is really the fly-fishing Promised Land. The trout here have a wonderful affinity for eating off the surface, a very visual element that delights most who enjoy the sport. But even when the fish feast on subsurface fare, these large and angry fish push the excitement level way beyond most expectations. The average size of fish, and more importantly their tenacity, surprises most first-time visitors.

These are wild trout, spawned in the cold mountain waters of the Upper Missouri and its tributaries, conditioned to be wary of strangers but very fond of the abundant and seemingly endless supply of aquatic insects that make their home in this very fertile tailwater fishery. This is a wonderful playground where trout fatten themselves on the rich and plentiful food, and fly fishers can test their fly patterns and skills against big brown and rainbow trout.

Tailwaters, those streams that flow out of dams, and the Missouri River specifically, tend to intimidate many anglers. Unlike freestone rivers, which are undammed, this river is like a huge spring creek where large boulders and other visible structure is mostly missing. Newcomers are sometimes daunted by its sheer size, and by what first appears to be a nondescript appearance. With few of the characteristics of classic trout water, it's often difficult to read. The truth is that the riffles, runs, and pools are all there, but they are subtle and you have to train your eye to look more closely. Rising fish are often very subtle when taking adult flies. It's what fly fishing should be—subtle, soft, and quiet.

This book will address how, when, where, and with what to fish the Missouri River in central Montana. It's about fly fishing for trout on the Blue Ribbon section between Holter Dam and the town of Cascade. It's about patterns that work and it's about how to fish those patterns. It's about leaving your troubles behind and enjoying the sport of fly fishing.

Turning leaves near the town of Hardy punctuate the blue sky of September.

Seasons of the Missouri

Montana is a wondrous place that I'm very proud to call home. It has become my wild and crazy friend who refuses to fit into a sports coat and tie. Instead, it lives a life free of rules and predictability—one day its serene and lovely, the next grim and angry. It has no alarm clock and you can wake up to its winter any month of the year. Its cologne is the sweet smell of sage and pine blended with fresh cut alfalfa or the aroma of newly fallen rain on a dusty road. Compared to the eastern seaboard, this is untamed country for the most part. You might share your piece of river shoreline with beaver and mink, but don't be surprised to see black bears eating chokecherries from the bushes that line the rivers.

Residents of this state can tell you what sort of weather there usually is in, say, June—but only the foolhardy believe that five-day weather forecast The Weather Channel puts out every hour. Hell, they don't even call us Montana, but rather "the northern Rockies." I'm not convinced they know we are not part of Canada. So, if you are planning a trip here, forget the wingtips and ties, and pack all the rest of the clothing you own.

In the State of Montana, virtually all lakes and many rivers are open year-round for fishing. The Missouri can be fished any month, even in winter for those hardy, or some would say "fool-hardy," enough to venture out. The weather is the deciding factor and not the season. It can be 50° F. in January and 45° in July and the local residents often leave their fleece and wool within reach all year long. It can also be -50° in January and 100°+ in July. This is a semi-arid climate with annual precipitation totals near 12 inches, but it's also a place of extremes, and that number can vary from drought to flooding. Check the local forecasts as well as the average temperatures and precipitation if you want, but come prepared for those extremes.

Summer

The running joke here in central Montana is "We have two seasons—winter, and those two days in July." Some years it's not really funny, but most years we begin our summer in earnest in June. That is also the month that has the highest average rainfall, so in wet years you might not have temperatures that you would call summer-like until July. Then the rain quits and the temperatures can reach into the 90s. An afternoon thunderstorm can cool it down into the 70s or even 60s, and I have guided on days in July when the daytime high was 45. But the norm is for hot and sunny days.

Tricos *(Tricorhythodes)* show up on the river as early as the middle of July, but normally a bit later. They will hatch almost every morning until the end of August or first part of September. You'll have to roll out of bed near sunrise to see the spectacle of mating swarms along the banks and the spinner falls that blanket the river. The PMD hatches continue in July and often into mid-August. Caddis and mayflies are present most days also. Casting hopper imitations along the banks in the late morning or afternoon will often entice large browns and rainbows up from the bottom where they are contently digesting the belly full of Tricos they sipped all morning. A nice juicy hopper might be a piece of apple pie à la mode for them—something they just can't resist, no matter how full they are.

Beetles, ants, and other terrestrials can also bring fish up when there hasn't been a rise for hours. Or fishing attractor patterns along the banks, especially with a nymph dropper, is often a productive way to spend the afternoon. Of course you might also choose to enjoy a nice streamside lunch and just watch the water go by.

Fall

Often by the end of September we will have seen our first snow or first frost. If the wind shifts from southerly to out-of-the-north, you'll feel a distinct chill in the morning air. The foliage along the banks turns to shades of yellow and red, and the leaves on the trees get noisy in the wind as they dry in preparation for the coming winter. The warm water, reacting to the cooler air, produces a smoke-like mist to greet the rising sun as it retreats farther and farther south, shortening the days. It's a magical time on the river—a time of change. The kids are back in school, vacations are over for the summer, the crowds along the river are thinning, and the fish know that the time to bulk up is now. Soon the food supply will dwindle back to tiny midges and the water temperatures will hover in the high 30s to low 40s. Nature is about to close the buffet line.

After the first frost or snow, the hopper fishing usually deteriorates dramatically. By the end of September the whispering mating swarms of Tricos are a faint memory, but tiny *Pseudos* and *Baetis* are still present and there is a newcomer on the block

Wade fishing on the Missouri is an easy task in most areas like this one at Mountain Palace.

who's HUGE! At first you just see or hear these bad boys around dusk. Then maybe one lands on an oar or the bank. This is the October Caddis hatch. No more #22 Tricos. These obese giants are #8s and #10s. They hit the water with the subtlety of an elephant fart, but trout will move in from long distances because their clumsiness is offset by what they have in size. As the buffet line is closing down, they bring out the prime rib to serve up to the winter's prisoners. This isn't a time for Weight Watchers, this is the time to gorge.

These lesser hatches can be sporadic and difficult to predict, but they can make you giddy. Often, the main part of the hatch happens after dark, but the fish remember and will usually hit a dry fly pattern in late afternoon without even one single natural in sight. The burnt orange bodies of the large naturals are a dead giveaway if you spot them along the banks.

The Missouri's water temperatures here, moderated by Holter Dam, can often stay warm when the air temperatures are well below freezing. The trout will continue to feed actively even when the guides on your rod are freezing up. The browns seem to be more receptive to spawning in the mainstem of the river, and this is when it happens. But many move out, leaving the predominant rainbows alone. This is also Wooly Bugger time.

Most years, winter will take a grip on the river sometime in November. In extreme years the daytime highs will be hovering around zero by mid-month, but many years it's 50s one day and 20s the next. Ice along the banks gets thicker and thicker, closing the curtain on the river. The river never freezes over completely close to the dam, but downstream of Mountain Palace the edge ice reaches out far from the bank, and slush flows down what little water is open.

Winter

From around Halloween until the end of March, trout subsist mostly on midges and various non-insect species like scuds, sowbugs, and blood worms. When the water temperatures are still rela-

The grade of the river changes near Pelican Point and slows to a meander.

9

tively warm in early November, or if an opportunity presents itself, they will eat larger fare like sculpins, leeches, and various baitfish.

For those typical winter months, it's always a treat to look at the weather forecast and see a day with highs in the 40s, sunny and without wind. These are typically the days when you'll find fish dimpling the surface eating midge clusters, but you're also likely to encounter many other fly fishers who suddenly came down with a 24-hour virus that prevented them from getting out of bed and off to work that day. Just be sure to wear plenty of sunscreen so you don't have to explain those raccoon eyes to your boss when you return to work after your miraculous recovery.

Dressing for cold weather fly fishing is an art form. While the air temperatures might be comfortably in the 40s, the water temperatures can pull heat away from your body, leaving your feet feeling like frozen stumps that really don't belong to your legs. Stepping from the river with wet felt soles onto shore ice is another hazard when your feet are numb. It's like trying to eat a sandwich when the dentist's novocaine is still in full force–not a good idea. A pair of studded wading boots will help keep you from taking that header. Many fly fishers used to use heavy neoprene in the winter and lighter weights in the summer. The same Gore-Tex® waders can be worn year-round by simply changing the layers worn underneath.

The good news is that you won't have to pack fifty pounds of flies into your vest because the selection is pretty fundamental. And that's a good thing since with all the fleece you have on, you're starting to look like the Michelin man with hives. Midge larva, pupae and dry fly imitations are the winter staple along with scuds, sowbugs, and the ubiquitous San Juan Worm. For most anglers, the mainstay is nymphing under an indicator this time of year, but keep your eyes open for those midday midge hatches that draw the fish into small groups of sipping risers called pods. When this happens have a good supply of LaFontaine Buzzballs or Griffiths Gnats.

Water temperature is a very important factor in a trout's feeding habits during the winter months. When the temperature is dropping in the late afternoon, the fish seem to either quit or slow down their already lethargic feeding. Trout will begin feeding on those days when the sun hits the river's substrate and the water begins to warm. The fly fisher's nearly numb feet won't feel this slight change, but the fish seize this time when their tiny prey starts to move. If casting dry flies to rising fish is what you are looking for, the window of opportunity is often very small this time of year. It takes the right condi-

The canyon ends near the Prewett Creek FAS and the views change with it.

tions of sun and temperature and the only hatch you are likely to see on the Missouri this time of year are midges.

The water this time of year is typically very low. Activity on the river is at a minimum as the osprey and other predators are gone, sunning themselves in warmer southern climates. Since a fly line can ice up quickly, your presentations might resemble an Atlantic naval battle, so a classic upstream presentation usually will do little more than scatter the fish like a bunch of toddlers at bath time. A better tactic is to get above them and cast downstream at 45° angle with slack line and a good reach cast. Then the first thing the fish sees is the fly and not your fly line or leader.

A reach cast is better shown than described, and most of the casting videos do a good job. Simply put, it's a conventional cast, made somewhat downstream, where the angler "reaches" upstream with the tip of the rod just before the fly hits the water. This effectively mends the line before it's on the water, compared to a traditional mend where the fly line is lifted upstream of the fly after it's on the water.

The takes are mostly subtle with these sippers and gulpers. Pause for a moment to allow the trout to close his mouth, and then set the hook by just lifting the slack from the fly line. You'll quickly snap your 4X or 5X tippet with an aggressive set and it's not necessary. Play the fish by coaxing him out of the current and then

Winter fishing offers fewer anglers and a welcome break from household chores for Dan Badovinac.

practice the methods described in the Catch and Release chapter of this book. A catch and release tool is almost a must this time of year. It allows you to release the fish without wetting your already cold hands.

Spring

When I think of Spring I think of wet snow falling on grass that's trying to green up. In Montana it may be the most unsettled time of the year for weather. Often the winds can be fierce and temperatures can easily go from 60s one day to 20s the next. This is *Baetis* weather.

These tiny mayflies start showing up on the lower river around the middle of April. The trout have spent all winter foraging on midges, and the much larger *Baetis* are often what will finally bring them to the surface en masse. You might also see sporadic hatches of March browns (*Rhithrogenia*). Unfortunately, these hatches can often coincide with the migration of the rainbows.

While some of the resident rainbows will make redds and

A springtime drop in atmospheric pressure can bring a storm on and sprinkle the landscape with snow or rain.

spawn in the river's mainstem, most move up the Dearborn and Little Prickly Pear rivers beginning in early April. It's quite a sight! Both of these tributaries are closed to fishing until the third Saturday in May, but you can walk their banks to watch the spawning migration. You may find thousands of trout swimming around, and sometimes leaping over, obstacles to reach some pre-appointed spot where they will begin the next generation. Usually by the end of the first week of May, many are moving back into the mainstem of the river and by the time the streams are open (the third Saturday in May), most, if not all, of the spawning is complete.

This migration doesn't mean that you can't catch fish on the Missouri. Often this is a good time to catch big browns. Just be sure to watch your step and, if you see those tell-tale light colored patches, especially on gravel beds, move to other water to avoid harassing the spawners. Remember, without a next generation, the fishing will go downhill quickly.

This is the time of year when the brown trout on the Missouri get really crazy. They will jump like rainbows on fire. Tail walks are common and broken tippet isn't unusual. They will often take streamers, and under the right conditions will even come up for midge or *Baetis* patterns, but on most days nymphing will be the most productive. Pink scuds, San Juan Worms, midge larva and pupae for nymphing, and dry cluster imitations, Adams and Hi-Vis Parachute patterns are good choices for top water. Around the middle of April, throw in some small Pheasant Tails, Lightning Bugs, RS-2s and my personal favorite, the Love Bug.

Bringing plenty of extra clothing and being prepared for any kind of weather allows you to enjoy the Missouri when there are fewer people and boats. This is pre-runoff time and, in most years, you won't see a lot of really muddy and heavy runoff conditions until around the end of May or the first part of June. In low-water years, it's unlikely that you'll see any real change in the river aside from a slight coloring of the water below the tributaries, but that often is brief and does not significantly affect the

fishing. In high-water years, except during those extreme years, casting Wooly Buggers to the banks from a drift boat will often solicit fierce strikes from winter-starved trout.

Late May is normally when runoff begins. It can happen overnight if the weather warms quickly or if it starts raining. Sometimes you'll see a Caddis hatch on the lower river just before runoff begins, but it's usually short-lived, as the muddy water from the tributaries during runoff will suppress the hatch as it cools the water of the mainstem. During June, especially in low-water years, the first pale morning duns can appear.

The quality of springtime fishing is directed by winter's snowpack. Near Stickney Creek, low springtime flows mean good fishing.

Two anglers enjoy the bullpen located just downstream of Holter Dam.
High springtime flows can put this island underwater.

Wade Fishing the Missouri

From time to time on the river I come across a spin or bait fisherman. It often brings me back to the time when I was fishing the Arkansas River near my hometown of Canon City, Colorado. I had this belief that the fish were holding just outside my casting range. Lots of them, probably hundreds, but maybe more, were quietly swimming and feeding and doing fish stuff, oblivious to the fact that I had just gotten another perfectly good hand-me-down, made by Garcia or Shakespeare. All I had to do is get the goods out to them. It became a war-like strategy to deliver the bait to the enemy using more and more firepower. It took a lot of lead to deliver that night crawler, and the heavy artillery I had in my tackle box was my newest stroke of youthful genius.

Weeks earlier, while digging through the good junk behind Jim's Tire and Gas, Griz and I discovered an inner tube that only needed minor patches. It was a reward as good as any buried pirate's treasure and would float us down the irrigation ditch by our houses when the August temperatures crawled into the 100s and the old farts in town were still debating whether to build us kids a new pool. There on the ground were all these crescent shaped chunks of metal with a small wing on it–wheel weights that were used to balance tires.

After picking up handfuls, we walked around the front of the station where guys in uniforms were racing around cars cleaning windows, pumping gas, and checking oil. Each of them had a rag hanging out of his pocket that lofted like eagle tailfeathers as they flew from the garage, where they smoked cigarettes while waiting for the next DING-DING signaling that the next customer had driven over that long rubber tube and was ready for service and Green Stamps. Griz and I used to run over that tube with our bikes, but mostly we weren't heavy enough to set off the bell unless we both piled on one bike. But then getting away before the guys could squirt us with water was a challenge.

On this day it was pretty busy and there were people waiting for service. The Texaco men were at full stride as they attacked the cars like an Indy pit crew. When I approached the first man with an outstretched hand full of wheel weights he only said "Not now kid!" So Griz and I sat on the little bench in front of the big glass windows and waited. We heard guys yelling "Two quarts Penz 10-30," or "The guy in the Pontiac got Ethel, not regular." We mostly knew what they were talking about but sometimes it would get technical and we had no clue. "Sounds like that Chevy pickup has a bad lifter."

When the tornado passed and the men began picking up stray oil cans that didn't make it to the trash or rags that dropped

Flocks of Canada geese populate the river in winter along with swans and other waterfowl. In spring their nests dot the shoreline.

"Will they melt?" I asked.

"Damned straight! Them's lead, but ya' got to get 'em real hot, and be damned careful, kid. Don't burn yer ol' man's garage down." There was no point in telling him that we didn't have a garage, but I needed more.

"How would you melt them?" We followed him as he walked into the garage lighting his cigarette, headed for the far wall. After slipping on heavy gloves he grabbed the OxyAcetelin torch and fired it up with a funny little tool that created a spark as it scraped metal across metal. Foof! and the torch was lit as he held the wheel weight with a pair of long pliers and put the torch to it. Almost immediately the lead started dripping on the metal bench where it splattered and turned into a solid again. Almost in unison, Griz and I said, "Wow!" We were witnessing a miracle of science. He turned off the torch and we were immediately inspired.

through the engine compartment onto the ground, Griz and I stood like hero-worshiping fans waiting for an autograph. As they were returning to the back of the garage to finish their smokes that had long since burned away in the ash tray, I extended my handful of wheel weights again to a man whose cigarette was stuck behind his ear like a pencil at the ready.

"Them is wheel weights. Whatcha gonna do with 'em?" he asked, bending down and retrieving the cigarette from behind his ear.

"Thanks mister." We grabbed our bikes and sped home to create our own magic. Eventually, we made crude molds and melted the lead into them with torches our dads used for plumbing.

We ended up with weights the size and mass of spark plugs that spooked every fish within a hundred yards when they landed on the water, making as much noise as a battleship anchor.

As the years went by I discovered that most of the fish were fairly close to shore, and that I was casting over them. I learned that the grass isn't always greener on the other side, and I learned that a delicate presentation catches more trout than massive firepower.

The Missouri River *(see map section starting on page 28)* has good genes. Its parents are the Madison, the Gallatin, and the Jefferson Rivers, which come together near the town of Three Forks. Twenty miles downstream it encounters its first dam—Toston. Toston is a minor dam and only one of many that the water will encounter on its way to the Mississippi River. In the event that you find yourself on a game show it might be helpful to know that the Missouri is the longest river in the United States at 2,714 miles. It ends up flowing into the Mississippi just north of St. Louis, Missouri. The Mississippi is a mere 2,350 miles.

Twenty-three miles downstream of Toston Dam, the river dumps into Canyon Ferry Reservoir near the town of Townsend. Canyon Ferry is a very large dam with often strong winds blowing across it. It took Lewis and Clark days to navigate this stretch in their dugout canoes, as there was no lake at the time. If you try a canoe adventure here, use extreme caution. This reservoir is really the southeastern end of a series of three dams. Directly to the northwest are Hauser and Holter dams. From Townsend to the face of Holter Dam is 66 river miles.

It is here, downstream of Holter Dam, where the Blue Ribbon

El Niño means above average temperatures and below average snowfall in Montana. It also means winter fishing with gloves.

section of the Missouri begins. It is also where the focus of this book begins. The Missouri's confluence is 108 miles to the southeast near the town of Three Forks, and traveling this far downstream the water has been moderated and filtered, creating an ideal habitat for trout. This section of river, from Holter Dam to the town of Cascade, is home to tens of thousands of trout. The populations of fish vary from high-water to low-water years, but they are always much higher than anywhere else on the river. These high numbers of trout, plus the consistently great hatches of aquatic insects, make this a dream come true for fly fishers.

Holter Dam is a hydroelectric dam without the usual radical flow fluctuations of power generating facilities. This offers the best of tailwater fly fishing opportunities. I have a love-hate relationship with dams. I've spent many hours standing below them casting tiny dry flies to anxiously waiting trout, but when I gaze up at the dams in the bright sunlight, they have faces only an engineer could love. Holter Dam is no raving beauty. Its broad girth of concrete and steel stands like the offensive line of an NFL team—big, ugly, and toothless, it rises up day in and day out to protect the throwing arm of the quarterback as he hurls missiles to anxiously waiting targets. If the dams fail in their duties, hell comes to dinner. And without the dams, many people are without electricity.

Holter Dam creates downstream tailwaters—very rich, albeit a bit unnatural, habitats. Controlled flow from the reservoirs creates a silted bottom in many parts of the river, and long, flowing aquatic grasses. These grasses not only give protection to the fish, but also provide a good home to aquatic insects. Tailwaters like the Missouri's have fewer numbers of different insects, but the ones that hatch, do so in massive numbers.

Summertime means warmer temperatures and hatches of mayflies and caddis.
This flat just above the Craig Bridge often is dotted with rising fish.

Holter Dam to Wolf Creek Bridge
2 MILES—SEE MAP PAGE 29

In the winter months, the section of river between Holter Dam and the Wolf Creek Bridge is especially productive because the dam moderates the water temperatures and keeps the water from freezing over. Generally, the most productive areas for nymphing seem to be where the water is moving at a moderate pace. The fish can get food without exerting a lot of energy and without having to move quickly. Riffles carry more food, but the speed is too much for the lethargic trout. The areas adjacent to riffles are good choices, especially for nymphing. When the winter midge hatch begins, you will often find the trout moving to slower water especially if there are eddies where the insects can collect in large numbers.

Cold springtime water temperatures won't much change where the trout hold. But they tend to feed more aggressively in faster-moving water. With the higher water temperatures and longer days come the *Baetis*. These mayflies, commonly known as a Bluewinged Olive, or BWO, seem to have an affinity for nasty weather. On the Missouri in general, if there is a springtime snowstorm, bundle up and fish this hatch. It's exciting and often long-lasting, and the fish seem to feed like they were just released from prison.

As the water warms, trout will generally hold in faster current where there is more oxygen. In the hottest part of summer, the coldest and most oxygenated water is near Holter Dam because the dam is releasing water from the bottom of the lake where it's the coldest.

As fall develops, the water temperatures drop with the colder nights and snows, but the fish don't seem to move into their winter patterns until the water temperatures drop into the mid-to low 40s. That might not occur until late November, or even December, depending on the weather.

When fishing from a drift boat, we normally are casting right up next to the bank because this is where the largest concentration of fish is often found. Yet, whenever I see people wade fishing, they always seem to wade out into the river as far as possible and then cast their flies even farther. Yes, there are places where the water isn't even covering your wading boot and in the middle of a sunny day there will be few fish in these very shallow areas. But, when a hatch is on, it's not unusual for very large fish to move into water that exposes their dorsal fins! It just makes sense to take a moment to look at the water before you crash into it like a linebacker going after a fumble.

It also makes sense to "fish your way out." When nymphing, this involves making a few casts, then taking a few steps out and making a few more casts. It's amusing for me to see someone crashing out into the river, notice fish scurrying everywhere, and announce, "Wow, there are fish everywhere," then continue their charge. Those fish will feed again, but they are now spooked. It will take some time to calm them down enough for them to resume their normal feeding.

When there is a visible pod of rising fish, take a moment to study the water to see what and how the fish are eating. Then, even if you can't identify the species with the correct Latin name, you can search your box for something of the correct size and silhouette. Start with a

pattern that is one size smaller than the natural. This is a good rule of thumb for a couple of reasons. The first is that most anglers will look at an insect, especially an adult with wings, and think it's bigger than the equivalent pattern because the wing is not factored into the size of the pattern. The pattern size is determined by the gap of the hook. What extends above the shank doesn't affect its size rating. The second reason is that within

Tricos love the Missouri and greet early rising anglers with pods of fish that chase these mayflies. Just be careful when you inhale.

19

every species of aquatic insect, there are size variations and, as humans, we naturally are drawn to the largest items. So we have a skewed idea about the size that would best mimic the naturals.

The two miles of river between the dam and the Wolf Creek Bridge are easily accessible. The dirt road on the west side goes up to the dam and a campground. The paved road on the east side follows the river for about a mile before it heads up to the reservoir. There are numerous places to park and fish—but be aware of the private land that is clearly marked and respect the rights of property owners generous enough to allow river access. Keep in mind that, in Montana, an orange fence post is legally a "No Trespassing" sign.

There are many easy-to-access wading spots on the Missouri. This one is about a mile upstream of Craig. Pelicans are also looking for rising fish.

Several small islands in this section are easy to wade when the flow out of Holter Dam is low or moderate. Always use caution, and don't let the easygoing flows of the Missouri trick you into complacency.

This section is by far the easiest to access for the wading angler. It's also likely to be the place to see a neoprene, fiberglass, or air mattress hatch.

Parking spots are very obvious on both sides of the river on this stretch and there are almost no bad fishing spots. The property owners are fly fisher friendly as long as you don't destroy fences or harass livestock, but be careful to park only in well-defined parking areas and don't block gates. There is a State campground on the west side of the river near the dam, and a Fishing Access Site (FAS) just upstream of the campground that serves as a boat launch and parking area. Keep in mind that these boat ramps are heavily used during the summer, and trying to fish from them won't be very peaceful.

From the Wolf Creek Bridge, the paved Recreation Road closely follows the Missouri River to just beyond Pelican Point, 25.5 river miles downstream. This was the old highway from Great Falls to Helena. Along this corridor are many places to park and fish, but generally the farther from the dam, the less river access there is. Stretches of river have small developments and houses; while Montana law permits you to walk the shoreline below the normal high water mark, you cannot cross private property to get to the river without landowner permission.

During Trico hatches the late sleepers not only miss the top-water action, they also miss the magic of early mornings on the river.

Wolf Creek Bridge to Craig
5.5 MILES–SEE MAP PAGE 29

The Wolf Creek Bridge to Craig section is 5.5 river miles and the Recreation Road closely follows the river on the east side. A Fishing Access Site with boat ramp and small campground is just below the bridge on the east side. A dirt road on the west side runs close to the river from about the halfway point to Craig. By far the easiest access is on the east side of the river.

road—as well as the area upstream—normally offer very high concentrations of trout.

About a mile and a half above Craig you will find a small white bridge and a large turnout. The bank drops sharply down to the river but you can walk upstream to get down to the water. There is a fairly good sized toilet bowl eddy here that attracts trout food and trout. The pods of feeding fish can be an amazing sight, a pod sometimes holding close to a hundred fish. Even the best of casters won't be able to reach the entire pod as there are a steep bank and even steeper drop-offs, making wading difficult.

The fishing upstream offers easier going. During low flows, the Missouri usually is shallow enough to wade to an island just across from the little white bridge. A few more islands rise upstream of it. If you plan your crossings, you can move from one island to another—but you'll be fighting the current whenever you move upstream. The reward is easy wading, and often a great evening hatch.

About three-fourths of a mile upstream of the Craig Bridge is a side channel that runs around a very large island. A small bridge, which used to be a railroad car, runs over the side channel to the island. The channel is usually very easy to wade during flows under 5,000 cfs, and during evening caddis hatches, can be very productive. You will have to walk a short distance from the Rec Road, and be sure not to block the rancher's gate with your truck.

At the Craig Bridge is another state campground with FAS/Boat Ramp, as well as many wading spots above, and even more below, the bridge. Parking at the boat ramp and then crossing the bridge and wading downstream can offer some really great fishing. But keep in mind that rising fish within casting dis-

In low flow years you can wade far out into the middle of the river. Here, the old quarry can be seen in the background.

Of the numerous pull-offs and wading opportunities on this stretch, one of the better ones is about 1.5 miles north of the Wolf Creek Bridge. This one has a nice walk-through fence. When the flows out of Holter Dam are 4,000 cfs or less, wading across to the island closest to the road isn't too difficult for a strong angler; the river will be about knee deep where the current is the strongest. Above 5,000 cfs, the water level can get as high as waist deep for a 6'- tall man and, with the added current, is dangerous for all but the very strongest. The second island toward the middle of the river cannot be reached by a wading angler even in the driest of years. But the side channel near the

tance of a campground get lots of pressure, and you may find that even your best presentation isn't good enough.

Most of the access on the west side of the river on this section is private, but look for one site near an old quarry. From Craig, drive south, or upstream, on the gravel road that parallels the railroad tracks, for approximately two miles, to where you'll see distinct parking places.

A series of islands and side channels here often offers wonderful top-water action during morning Trico and evening caddis hatches. It's also great nymphing water as the current is almost perfect for subsurface flies.

Craig to Dearborn

6 MILES–SEE MAP PAGE 30

Aside from the area below the Craig Bridge, wading opportunities close to the road are non-existent for the next mile or so as the Recreation Road moves away from the river. The west side is lined with private property and steep banks. There is no public road on the west side except the Interstate and that, for the most part, isn't a viable alternative because of the lack of parking and the long walk through private property. For most of the east bank above where the Interstate crosses both the river and Rec Road, the bank is steep,

but if water flows are low you can usually wade far enough from the bank to get a decent back cast.

Your reward for risking knee surgery on the rocky bank may be some really nice pods of anxious fish. Oftentimes, huge pods of trout will congregate along this bank, feeding on the "hatch du jour" that seems to cling to the safety of nearby willows. But numer-

Sudden spring snow or rainstorms turn the Dearborn River into a muddy mess. The dams on the Missouri can often filter the water. The contrast is evident where the Missouri and Dearborn meet.

Brown trout, while not the predominant species on the river, grow larger than the rainbows. Big males are rarely caught eating Tricos, but will take a well-presented hopper pattern.

ous cut-outs for parking mean that this road sees a lot of summer-time traffic. Many fishermen are distracted by hatches and rising fish while driving, so be careful when opening your car door.

Not too far below the Interstate bridge (**1**) begins another series of houses and cabins that extend to the Stickney Creek FAS/Boat Ramp, which is 2.5 miles from Craig. Here is another state campground and picnic area, but also a great jump-off point for wading anglers. The island across from the boat ramp is easy to wade to in low-water years, but cross at the very top of the island for safety, and fish the side channel down. You can fish the side channel from the road side of the Missouri, although thick willows make it like trying to navigate a rush-hour Tokyo sub-way with a fully strung fly rod.

The west side of the river here is private ranch land, often with steep cliffs. The railroad tracks run along the river and through long tunnels that could turn your trek into a cartoon where the frantic fisherman is being chased by an angry train.

The next FAS/Boat Ramp is Spite Hill, only a mile down-

stream from Stickney, but here more houses block access to the river. After Spite, the Rec Road is very close to the river, but stepping off this long riprap bank will put you in over the logo on your waders in most spots. The fish, especially brown trout, seem to like hugging this bank. It is not, however, the easiest place for wade fishing. If you walk downstream to just about where you could com-fortably fish, you'll find a row of houses that goes all the way to the Dearborn FAS/Boat Ramp.

You'll see the Dearborn River flowing into the Missouri on the west side. A railroad bridge crosses the Dearborn, and the Interstate bridge (**2**) goes over the Missouri.

Dearborn to Mountain Palace
8 MILES–SEE MAP PAGE 31

For the next couple of miles, the east side of the river isn't too wader-friendly. It's mostly private property until you see where the river braids around numerous islands. There you will find many spots to park and wade. Across the river on the west side are anoth-er state campground and FAS/Boat Ramp. This is Mid-Cañon Campground. To get there, leave the Interstate at the Dearborn exit, then turn east onto the dirt road, and follow the signs. If you are on the east side of the river, you'll have to drive back to Craig (about 8 miles) or drive north on the Recreation Road about 5 miles to the Canyon Access in order to get on the Interstate.

Both up- and down-river from the campground are easy to wade, and frequently you'll find rising fish, especially during the early morning Trico hatches of July through early September. In low-water years you can sometimes wade across to the islands, but the current is pretty swift and the rocks slippery. Your best bet is to fish down to the Interstate bridge (**3**); it's easy to wade and the fish are usually cooperative.

The adventurous can continue below the bridge, but a rock

wall that extends down to the water will stop you. You are now forced to turn back by a railroad tunnel, both dangerous and illegal to walk through.

The east side of the river, across from Mid-Cañon, has a steep riprap bank and an even more abrupt drop-off close to the shore that extends until just before the next bridge (**3**). Here the bank levels out a bit and the Missouri is fishable for a small distance. Below the bridge the shore soon turns into private property for the next mile or so, until you get downstream of the next Interstate bridge (**4**). Then, another riprap bank, but this one is not nearly as high or steep. The drop-off in the water is severe, though, and the main current runs right along the bank making it hazardous to the wading angler.

Just before the next bridge (**5**), (named the Gary Cooper Bridge because the actor's father, a Helena judge, had a ranch in the area), the river flattens out again for a short space. Below the bridge are more houses and private property, with very few places to access the river until you get to Mountain Palace. The Missouri's west side isn't really viable here for those without a boat or raft. Much of the shoreline is either private or accessible only by walking for miles.

Mountain Palace to Pelican Point

6 MILES—SEE MAP PAGE 32

Except for the two miles between Mountain Palace and the next campground/Fishing Access Site/Boat Ramp at Prewett Creek, this stretch of the Missouri offers very few places to easily access the river. The remainder of this six-mile stretch is dotted with shoreline houses and some of the steepest and highest cliffs on the Missouri River, which can be viewed from Prewett Creek. You'll often see golden and bald eagles riding the thermals or perching on these cliffs, and occasionally a mountain goat will be balanced on cliffs better suited for winged creatures.

The best fishing opportunities are between Mountain

Palace and Prewett Creek. An island sits just across from the boat ramp at Mountain Palace, but wading across the side channel should be done only by the very strongest of waders, and at very low flows. This current is very swift, and there are many subsurface obstacles. The good news is that the fishing in the side channel is very productive and very wadeable so risking a "dip in the cold pool" isn't necessary. The Recreation Road will be above you with a steep bank and private property for some of the half mile of shoreline that you can fish upstream from the boat ramp.

Summertime usually finds rising fish in view of the parking

The canyon section offers riffles and broken water where attractor patterns can often draw bottom nymph feeders to the top in spectacular fashion. The canyon walls probably watched Lewis and Clark as well.

lot, but you are likely to have lots of the usual campground company. Many dogs have an inherent instinct to retrieve anything you throw into the water, including a #22 Parachute Adams. Salmonoids, on the other hand, have an inherent instinct to scatter away from big, four-legged swimmers with large teeth. Trying to get someone else's dog to not retrieve your cast is always an interesting endeavor.

Below the Mountain Palace campground is a very high cliff that extends down to the water. This makes a great diving platform for summertime teenagers, but trying to lift a two-pound

Dave Payne in the broken water between where Sheep Creek enters the Missouri and Halfbreed Rapids. While not the easiest place to access for the wading angler, the rewards can be great.

flailing rainbow thirty feet in the air on a 5X tippet probably isn't going to have a happy ending for either you or the fish. The next half mile down to where the Rec Road crosses the river is all private anyway. We call this bridge the "Untouchables Bridge" because a scene from the movie The Untouchables was filmed here. Sean Connery and Kevin Costner played the good guys who shot it out with Al Capone's gang. The west side of the bridge was supposed to be Canada, and the Mounties came charging out of the hills to aid the FBI.

You probably won't find any Mounties or FBI agents unless you bring them with you, but you will likely find a really nice place to wade and fish on this west side of the river all the way to the Prewett Creek campground, about a mile downstream. Parking is plentiful off the Rec Road, which is now on the west side of the river, or at the campground. Often, this is great hopper territory in the hot days of July and August.

After the Prewett Creek campground there are very few accessible opportunities until you reach Pelican Point. But from Pelican Point you can walk back upstream for a mile or so, and there are plenty of easy wading spots. The river takes on a more freestone look after it exits the canyon just above where the Interstate crosses the river for the last time (6). The banks are less steep, and dotted with willows, and the river becomes shallower in most places and much easier to wade. The problem for the wading angler is access. The first mile or two below the mouth of the canyon has many houses. To access the Missouri from the east side means driving all the way to Cascade, crossing the river, and then driving back on a dirt road that will take you almost to the Interstate bridge and two sets of river rapids. All the land on that side of the river is private ranch land. Ask permission if you decide to try this adventure.

Pelican Point to Cascade

8.5 MILES–SEE MAP PAGE 33

This section is not really viable for the wading angler who wants to park his vehicle and walk to the river. For most of this stretch, the Interstate moves away from the river on the west side, and the Recreation Road runs west of the Interstate. Private ranchland, houses, long walks, and no parking make this a section to stay away from if you are afoot. This is almost always the windiest place on the 36 miles of river between Holter Dam and Cascade. The river now runs out onto the Montana plains, and the only thing slowing the wind down is wheat fields and cows.

Getting to the river at Pelican Point FAS is easy, but from this point downstream private property acts as a barrier to the wading angler. The river slows here as it continues its long journey to the Mississippi.

The Blue Ribbon Stretch
of the Missouri River
HOLTER DAM TO CASCADE—35.5 MILES

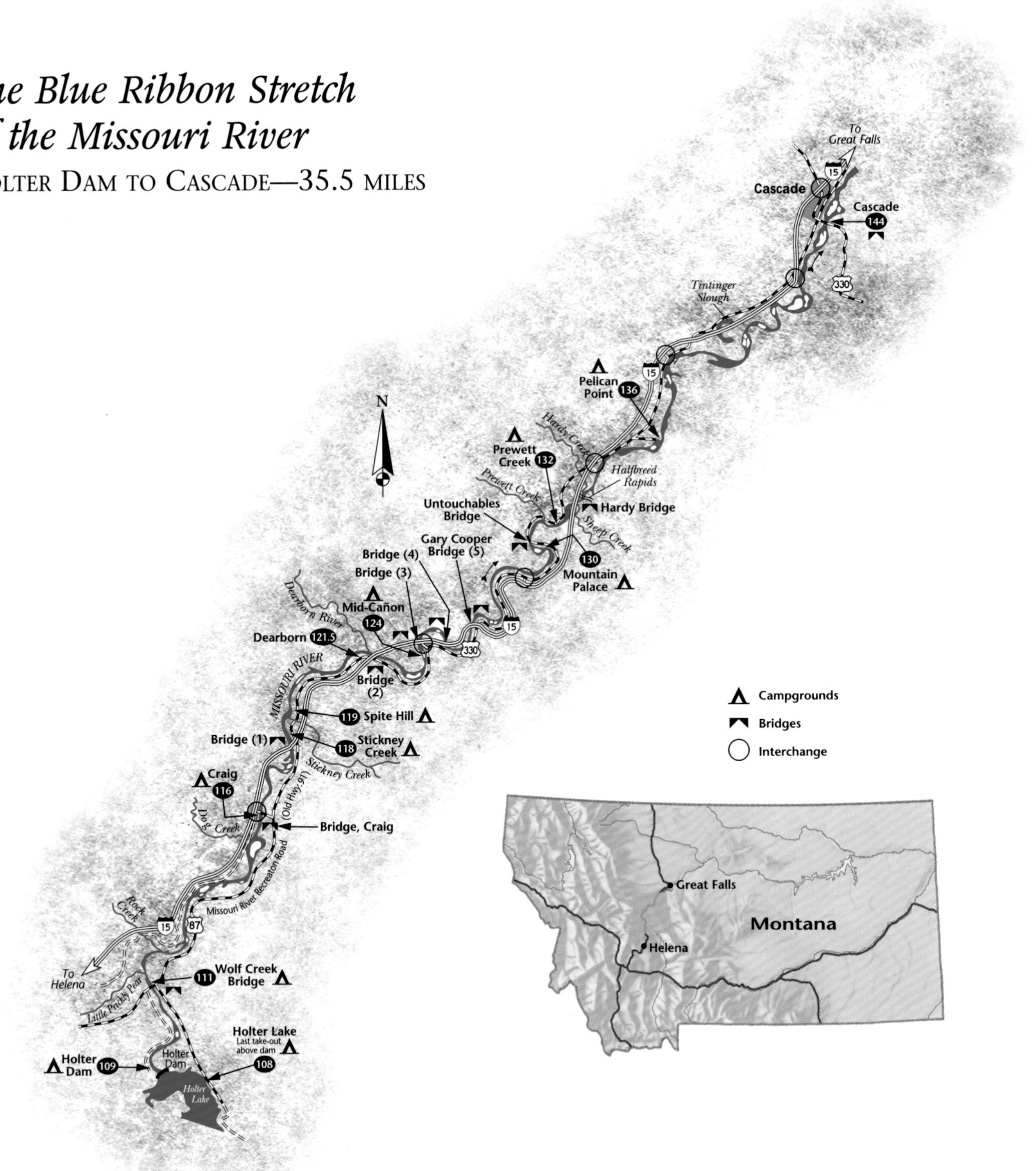

To Great Falls

Cascade

Cascade 144

330

Tintinger Slough

15

Pelican Point 136

Prewett Creek 132

Halfbreed Rapids

Hardy Creek

Prewett Creek

Untouchables Bridge

Hardy Bridge

Gary Cooper Bridge (5)

Sheep Creek

Bridge (4)

Bridge (3)

130

Mountain Palace

Dearborn River

Mid-Cañon

124

15

Dearborn 121.5

330

Bridge (2)

MISSOURI RIVER

119 Spite Hill

Bridge (1)

118 Stickney Creek

Stickney Creek

Craig 116

Dog Creek

Bridge, Craig

Missouri River Recreation Road (Old Hwy. 91)

15 87

Rock Creek

To Helena

Little Prickly Pear

Wolf Creek Bridge 111

Holter Lake
Last take-out above dam 108

Holter Dam 109

Holter Dam

Holter Lake

N

Legend
- △ Campgrounds
- ►◄ Bridges
- ○ Interchange

Great Falls

Helena

Montana

Holter Dam to Craig

7 MILES

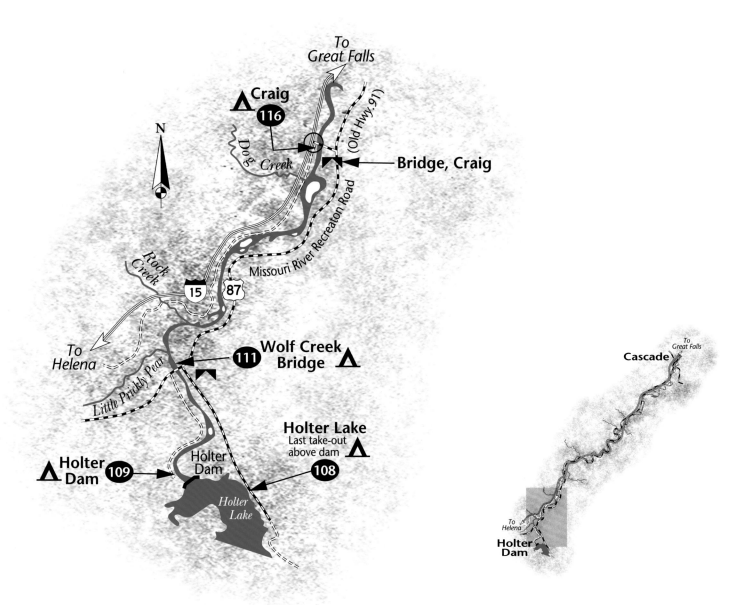

To
Great Falls

▲ **Craig**
116

N

Dog Creek

(Old Hwy. 91)

Bridge, Craig

Rock Creek

Missouri River Recreaton Road

15 **87**

To
Helena

Wolf Creek
Bridge ▲
111

Little Prickly Pear

Holter Lake
Last take-out
above dam ▲

▲ **Holter**
Dam
109

Holter
Dam

108

Holter
Lake

To
Great Falls

Cascade

To
Helena

Holter
Dam

Craig to Mid-Cañon
8 MILES

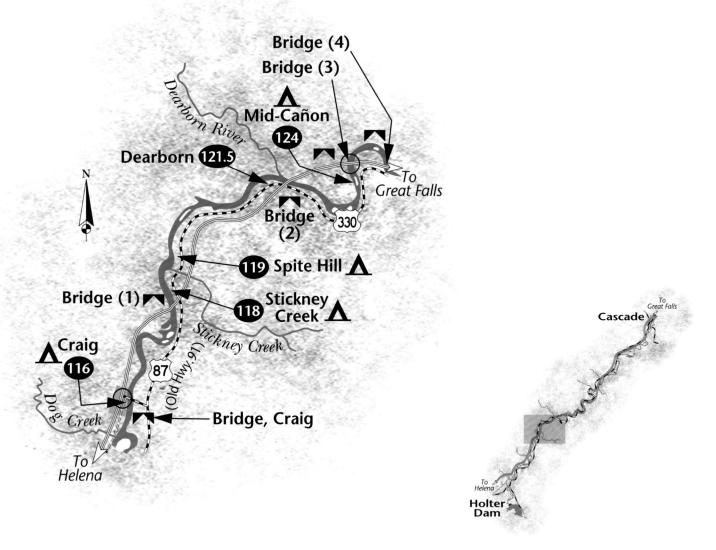

Bridge (4)

Bridge (3)

Mid-Cañon
124

Dearborn **121.5**

Dearborn River

N

To
Great Falls

Bridge
(2)

330

119 Spite Hill

Bridge (1)

118 Stickney
Creek

Stickney Creek

Craig
116

87 (Old Hwy. 91)

Dog Creek

Bridge, Craig

To
Helena

Cascade

To
Great Falls

To
Helena

Holter
Dam

Mid-Cañon to Mountain Palace

6 MILES

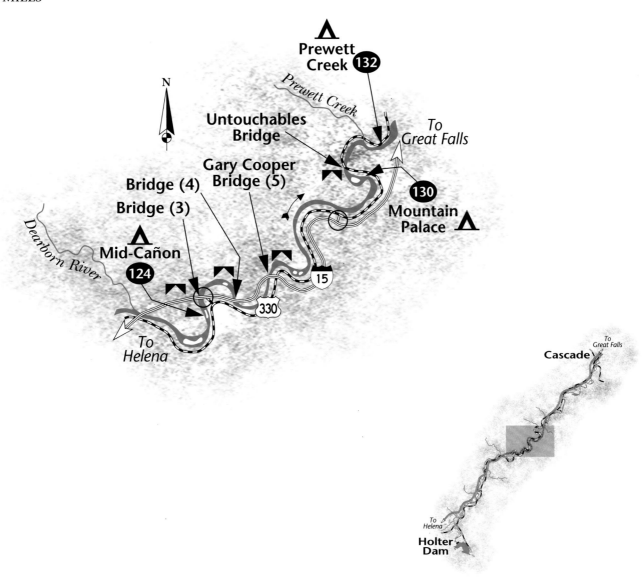

Mountain Palace to Pelican Point

6 MILES

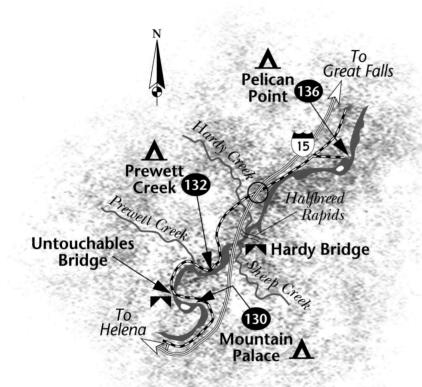

Pelican Point to Cascade

8.5 MILES

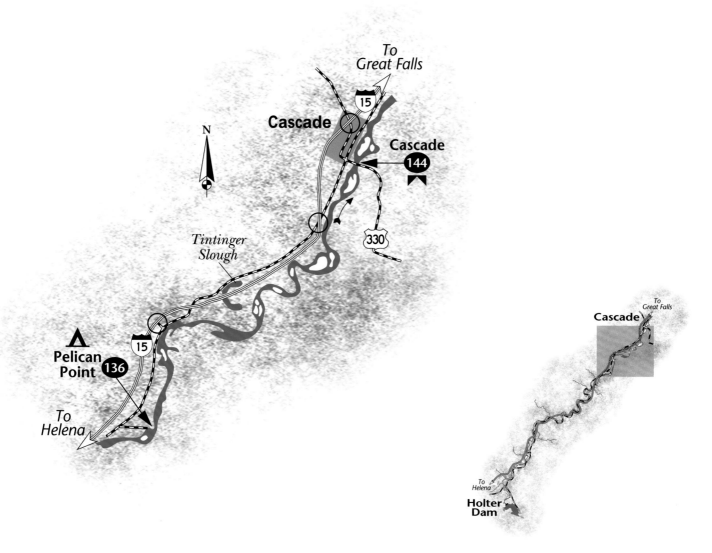

To
Great Falls

15

Cascade

Cascade

144

*Tintinger
Slough*

330

N

136

**Pelican
Point**

15

To
Helena

Cascade

To
Great Falls

To
Helena

**Holter
Dam**

The serenity of an early launch gives you time to observe the hatches and the fish. This FAS at the Wolf Creek Bridge is one of the most popular.

Floating the Missouri

My love affair with boats began a long time ago when I fished with Grandpa and Dad from Grandpa's aluminum boat. It had a small Johnson motor and I really liked the smell of the water plus gas mixed with oil. There was something almost mystical about heading out across a lake in the early morning before anyone else was out. Oftentimes the noise spooked deer as they drank from the water's edge, and they would run into the woods. Waterfowl would fly away as we approached. I loved to watch the ducks and geese as they seemed to run atop the water with their wings flapping. When they became airborne their wings shifted to a slower, more methodical rhythm. In the boat we mimiced them as we seemed to be flying across the water like free birds. I loved to sit in the bow and smell the humid morning air, rich with the scent of the water and woods. I would hear the boat cutting through the still water. I had my dad and my grandpa, my two invincible guardians, a lunch made by Mom and Grandma, a bucketful of freshly dug worms, and the wind in my face. Life was very good.

Eventually my dad bought a boat as well. It was a 16-foot aluminum, just like Grandpa's, but without a motor. He taught me how to row by picking out a place on the shore and keeping the stern aligned with it. We'd put it into some ice-cold Colorado lake, where we could hardly sit on the metal seats without a cushion because the cold would move through the metal. Without the motor it was just the creak of the oarlocks as we glided across the lake. God, I loved that boat.

I joined the Navy five days after I turned 18 so that I could get paid for being on a boat or ship. While I spent a hell of a lot more time cleaning and painting them, I did indeed get my wish. I again put myself on the bow of a ship and listened as she cut through the water, while I watched dolphins and flying fish dart and jump, playing with their very large newfound friend.

Since then I've bought and sold a dozen or so driftboats and rafts. I've yet to own a boat with a motor because the serenity of whispering water moving under me is so compelling. Combining fly fishing and floating seems like such a perfect marriage.

For the floating angler, there are numerous opportunities not available to the wading fly fisher. Drift boats are ideal for this river, but rafts work well also, and several shops along the river rent both. While some anglers choose to use float tubes or personal pontoons, these can be tough to navigate, especially for the beginner. Some very heated arguments have resulted when a tuber floated into wading anglers because the current was too strong for his fins. Drifting out of control through someone's pod of rising fish isn't a way to make friends on any river. The wind on the Missouri will only add to navigation problems.

Fishing from boats has been done for thousands of years. The materials used to build boats have changed, along with the design, and the drift boats used today on Western rivers are a result of running dories on rivers and oceans all over the world.

At first glance, the beginner will see a drift boat as nothing more than a row boat, and in some ways that is correct. Drift boats are designed and constructed for running rivers, with the

Floating offers the angler access to water that is nearly inaccessible otherwise. The high vertical walls at the end of the canyon can only be fished from a boat. The islands below it are mostly adjacent to private property.

bow and stern higher than the middle of the boat. So the section right below the rower is the part that sits the lowest in the water. When you go through rougher or shallower water, the boat will ride up and over the waves.

But the big equalizers are the current and the wind. Rowing on a lake with no wind, where mistakes are forgiven, is pretty easy to learn. Rowing drift boats on a river can be frustrating to the beginner, but it can also be dangerous. If you rent a boat, insist on some instruction before you launch.

Float fishing offers the angler considerable advantage. Standing in a knee brace gives a height advantage that allows you a better view of the fish, and also helps to keep your back-cast higher. More water can be covered, and this offers the opportunity to see parts of the river that may not be accessible to the wading angler. But one of the greatest advantages is that you can fish with your friends. While wade fishing, you normally see your companions periodically to ask how they are doing or when to break for lunch. While floating, you can share the experience. It affords the luxury of taking more than one rod, and many boats offer storage for fully strung rods so that you can switch from nymphing to dry fly fishing in seconds. But whether you are buying a boat, renting one for the day, or riding in one while a guide rows, you should familiarize yourself with them and their functions.

On most streams the fish spend a great deal of time near the banks of either the river or islands. When hatches occur, the insects journey to dry land as quickly as possible to avoid waiting mouths, and that means they land in the brush at the river's edge. Often they will mate here, and some will invariably fall back into the water. Fish become conditioned to look here because this is where their food spends most of its adult time. Hoppers, beetles, and other terrestrials also are found close to the flora. With a drift boat, you are most often casting fairly close to the shoreline. A wading angler has to get out into the main current and cast back toward shore to accomplish this. What's ordinary from a drift boat is often impossible or dangerous without one.

Boating Tips and Safety

With boats come certain safety considerations. When you get into a car, it doesn't move until you start it and drive. A drift boat is sitting on water and, when you get in or out, it moves—and it moves three dimensionally. This is where most falls take place. If you step out of a drift boat one leg at a time, as soon as your foot hits the river bottom it takes the weight off the boat and the boat will rise and often move away from you. Then you try to lift the leg still in the boat. At this point, if people haven't taken a header already, many will grab the gunwale for support. The boat then moves toward them, and the foot in the water goes under the boat and they either fall into the water or desperately hang on the gunwale like a giant sea slug clinging to a whale.

The solution is simple: exit the boat with both feet at the same time by sitting on the knee brace or gunwale and swinging both feet over. Hang on with your hands, and when both feet are on the river bottom, simply stand up. If you are floating with a guide, ask him about his boat, or wait until he drops the anchor and exits the boat. If he disappears into the water, stay in the boat.

If you are renting a boat, ask questions before you launch. In

Driftboats not only allow you easy passage to islands, but because of the Montana stream access laws, you can fish or wade anywhere below the normal high water mark.

Montana there are lifejacket and spare oar requirements and you should know where the safety gear is prior to launch, as well as how to handle the boat. Ask at the rental shop, or go to www.fwp.state.mt.us/

If you are in the boat with only one other angler, make certain that he is in the bow. Putting the lone angler in the stern raises the bow, drops the stern, and makes rowing and steering a nightmare. If you have one very heavy angler and one very light angler, the effect is the same if the heavier one is in the stern. The boat is best balanced when the most weight is in the bow. With rafts, this is much less of a consideration.

The key to safely navigating any stronger water is to go through bow first and not broadside. Going through broadside can take on water that could swamp the boat. If you are going to hit subsurface objects, the least amount of damage will be done by riding up and over it bow first. Broadside collisions can crush or even puncture the toughest of hulls.

Rookies sometimes panic and drop the anchor in heavy current or white water. Things are happening too fast for them to react and this seems to be a good idea. Often this results in a swamped boat. What happens is when the anchor sets on the bottom, often jammed into one of the many rocks that are causing the white water, the bow lifts, the stern drops and water comes rushing over the stern's transom. In seconds the boat is

underwater. As a safety precaution, don't tie a knot on the end of the anchor rope. If you ever get in this situation you can release the anchor rope and be on your way with only a small amount of water to bail out of the boat. You will lose your anchor and rope, but it's a small price to pay to prevent swamping and the subsequent frantic swim for gear and, possibly, someone's life.

When approaching a take-out or landing spot, use the stern to steer, and gently move toward the shallow water near shore, and then drop the anchor when the water is shallow enough to exit the boat. Pull the boat's stern onto the shore and lift the anchor onto solid ground. If the current is very swift, pull the boat farther onto the shore and/or pull more anchor rope out and drop it farther up the bank. Swimming after an empty drift boat is about as much fun as dropping an anchor on your foot.

Many first-timers want to approach a landing with the bow first by rowing forward. The speed of the current combines with the added velocity of the rower pushing forward and the result is that either the target landing is missed or it's hit with the velocity of a Smart Bomb, and with similar results. Using the stern to steer, and back rowing, is the only reasonable way to safely land a drift boat in most rivers.

Float Fishing

Fly fishing from a drift boat or raft is different than wade fishing, but with a little bit of knowledge and experience it can offer you a chance to fish water you could otherwise view only from a distance. There are some trade-offs but the benefits are wonderful. Some floaters use the boat only as a means to get from one

Driftboats also offer the opportunity to carry additional rods and a nice lunch for those lazy, but spectacular fall days. Sometimes just sitting back and enjoying the views is a good break.

wading spot to the next. Others rarely leave the boat and cover long distances, but the options available are much greater than those of wade fishing from shore.

Float fishing adds other elements for anglers to consider. When wading, errant casts might end up in the willows behind you or maybe in your hat, but normally you don't have two other people you could touch with your rod tip. In a drift boat or raft, you generally are in close proximity to the rower and the other angler. Safety becomes an issue because hooks obviously are sharp, and falling out of a boat can hurt.

One person rows while the anglers in the bow and stern, fish. The bow angler cannot see behind him too well, so it's the stern angler who must decide when to cast and when to wait. If both anglers are casting in a parallel plane, flies and lines will not tangle, but whenever casting gets away from parallel, trouble lurks and tangles can resemble macramé done jointly

Jill Oie takes the time to work some rising fish at the Mountain Palace FAS. It's always nice to give the rower an opportunity to stretch and cast.

by a cat and a toddler. Ideally, and in most situations when the rower is slowing the boat, the bow angler will cast slightly downstream at about the ten o'clock position and the stern angler will match that angle. A reach cast (*see* Seasons of the Missouri: Winter) will prove very valuable here. It will enable you to have longer drag-free drifts. If you notice that you are putting down rising fish well ahead of the boat, the bow angler should cast even farther downstream. If this doesn't work, the best solution is to anchor the boat and carefully wade fish. Wading lowers your profile and makes you less visible to the fish. If the rower holds the boat stationary, cast as if you were wade fishing.

The boat's knee brace is useful in that it gives you stability while casting, but it's also a great safety device. If you are standing out of the knee brace and the rower makes a sudden move to avoid an obstacle, or if the other angler makes an unexpected move or an aggressive hook set, you could find yourself tumbling into the water or another part of the boat. If you are standing away from the centerline of the boat, rowing and controlling the boat becomes more difficult for the rower.

A boat's *chine* is where the side and the bottom of the boat intersect. Many manufactures will keep this angle sharp to make the boat more maneuverable. When someone stands near the gunwale or moves decisively off centerline, the chines, with the current pushing against them, act as rudders and steer the boat.

Guides day off! Gary Fritz, one of the best outfitters on the river, takes a day off with Dave Payne, a local guide. Getting out of the boat to wade fish allows these anglers the opportunity to make multiple casts near the old quarry.

have to back row against the current to slow the boat. If you hook up the fish of a lifetime, the rower can help ease the strain on your tippet by moving the boat toward the fish if it heads downstream, or back rowing to keep it from heading upstream. After a hookup, a good rower will also try to maneuver the boat into slower water. This helps the angler to take the current out of the equation.

As you drift down the river, the pace is faster. You often won't get a second cast at a particular rising fish. The secret is to look where you are going to fish instead of where you've been. Casting back upstream, unless the rower is holding the boat stationary, will normally increase the drag on your flies since the boat is pulling you downstream. Look ahead for rising fish or likely holding areas, and time your casts accordingly.

Most rafts and some drift boats do not have knee braces. Casting is done while seated. This makes it very important to keep your casts high. Getting in and out of these craft is easier, as they sit closer to the water, but the two-feet-at-one-time method still applies.

The rower then has to compensate to keep the boat under control. Besides putting yourself in jeopardy, standing out of the knee brace makes the rower have to move the boat to compensate for your weight instead of putting you in a better position to catch fish.

The rower is key to successful float-fishing. If the fish you see rising are out of your casting range because the boat is too far away, you cannot deliver the fly. If the boat is too close, the fish are spooked. Maintaining an optimum speed gives the anglers time to make good, accurate casts, and this means the rower will

The toughest thing for first-time rowers to master is controlling speed and direction. While in a motorboat, you steer with the bow by changing the position of the motor, which acts like a rudder. While rowing a drift boat or raft, the rower faces downstream, looks over the bow and steers the boat with the stern. To move the boat to the right, turn the stern no more than a 45° angle to the right and row into the current. To slow the boat, row

The Missouri is much like a giant spring creek. Its flows are moderated by Holter Dam located two miles upstream from the Wolf Creek Bridge. Springtime temperatures warm the water and make the hatches and fish more active.

harder into the current. Turning the boat more than 45° increases the amount of hull subject to the push of the current and will often let the current take control.

Varying currents and eddies will try to move the boat in directions other than straight downstream. The rower's job is to try to keep the boat parallel to the shoreline, and at a distance that allows the two anglers to comfortably cast to rising fish or likely holding spots. Repositioning the boat, as well as making normal boat movements, needs to be slow and subtle.

"Back rowing" is a good technique for avoiding obstacles. It may be a rock visible above the surface or hidden just below. It could be a wading angler, or another boat that is anchored or moving slower than you, or maybe something very solid like a bridge column. Point the bow at the obstacle, the stern away from it, and row like you are trying to go back upstream. It's a good idea to begin this maneuver well before you are close to the object. With the current moving you toward the obstacle, it may take more work—and time—than you anticipate. The downstream floaters and the waders have the right of way. If you are upstream, it is your responsibility to avoid hitting them.

Over time, the shape of the river will change and what once was a shallow riffle will eventually become deeper as the water wears away the rock and gravel. High-water years can achieve this even faster. Water released from Holter Dam is usually pretty consistent during low-water years, but in high-water years, especially during runoff, it can vary widely. When floating this or any unfamiliar river, there are certain things to look for. Shallow areas are generally pretty obvious because that is where the water is riffling. The first time you float a particular section, it's a good idea to stop and check out these areas. Some side channels on the Missouri are tough to navigate when the water flows from Holter are below 4,000 cfs. This Blue Ribbon section also holds two sets of small rapids near Hardy Creek.

Not all sections of the river have the same number of FASs. This section between Pelican Point and the town of Cascade goes almost 9 miles between boat launches.

Fishing Access Sites (FAS)

The Montana Department of Fish Wildlife and Parks has constructed and maintains many Fishing Access Sites (FAS) on the Missouri and other rivers in the state. These are really just boat ramps. Some are well built of concrete, others are merely dirt and rocks cleared of willows and brush, but all are collection points for anglers.

At times, some floaters are trying to take their boat out while others are trying to put theirs in. Some floaters will drop off their boat and then have a friend follow them downstream to the take-out point where they will park their car and trailer, then ride back with the friend to the put-in. While they were gone, several boats may have launched and if all of them had to move the original boat to put theirs in, there might be some nasty notes left on the boat. Some floaters will back their boat trailer down the ramp and then have a cup of coffee or leisurely rig up their boat and rods while others are waiting anxiously to put their boats in the water.

Fly fishing is many things to many people, but I know of no one who wants to begin a day of fishing with a heated shouting match with another floater. Be considerate. If you put your boat in and are not going to launch immediately, move your boat out of the way. Rig up your boat and rods away from the ramp, so that when it's your turn, you can put in and launch quickly. The same applies at the take-out point. Washing your boat at the end of the day prevents it from staining, but cleaning your boat while blocking the ramp isn't going to win you any friends.

Drifters nearing the Little Prickly Pear Creek will find good fishing all the way to Craig. This section has no white water, even in high-water years.

How many miles to cover in one day depends on several factors. If your style is to stay in the boat and keep moving, you'll want to do a longer float of around 10 miles or so. But water flow will have a big influence on how fast you are drifting. Higher flows will move you downstream much faster than lower flows. On the Missouri, low flow is less than 4,000 cfs discharged from Holter Dam. Moderate flows are in the 5,000 to 6,000 cfs range, and high flows are in the 9,000 to 11,000 cfs range. Above 13,000 cfs the fishing gets pretty spotty unless you spend a great deal of time on the Missouri. Anything above 16,000 cfs is approaching flood stage.

A good rule of thumb is if the flow is moderate, and you'd like to do a float where you get out on different islands to wade fish occasionally and then drift fish your way from one island to another, a float of six to eight miles is probably an eight- or nine-hour day. But the other factor is the rower. Rowers who back row often, to give the anglers a better opportunity at either rising fish or choice spots, are going to be moving at a slower pace than those who just let the current push the boat downstream.

Moving your vehicle and trailer from the launch site to where you will take out is called a shuttle. You can do your own if you have an extra car and driver, throw a bicycle in either the boat or the car to get back, hitchhike, or simply bring an extra set of keys, give the keys and some money to the nice people at one of the local shops, and they will move your vehicle and trailer while you are fishing. Since these shuttle drivers are unfamiliar with your vehicle, it's a good idea that, after putting your boat in, you back your rig in at the parking area. That way they can simply drive it straight out.

Holter Dam to Craig

7 MILES—SEE MAP PAGE 29

The Fishing Access Site is just below the dam on the west side

Many islands dot this stretch between the dam and the town of Craig. Some areas are easy for the wading angler and care must be taken to give waders a wide berth.

of the river two miles upstream of the Wolf Creek Bridge. It's a little rough but not very steep. There is usually ample parking.

If you look up toward the dam you will see a cable that stretches across the river with warnings about not going above the cable. Take these warnings to heart, since there are easier ways to donate money to the State of Montana than paying a fine to the Department of Fish, Wildlife and Parks (FWP). Keep in mind the requirements for safety gear on your boat.

Whenever water is released from the dam not to go through the hydroelectric plant, an alarm sounds for 30 seconds on, 60 seconds off, then 30 seconds on again—five minutes before any water is released through the waste gates.

This section of the river between the dam and the Wolf Creek Bridge historically has the highest concentrations of fish. It also typically has the highest concentration of anglers. Since there are roads on both sides of the river, and easy access to the water, plus a campground just below the FAS, you might wonder if you have somehow been transported to a Pennsylvania chalk creek on opening day. One great thing about floating is that if you launch and there are more people than a Super Bowl tailgate party, you can float downriver to a less crowded section. Typically the most crowded area in this stretch is right around the FAS.

For the first two miles, it doesn't seem to matter where you fish—there are fish, and big fish, just about everywhere. Right in the middle of the river, numerous weed beds offer food, a current-break, and protection from predators. These areas are anomalies for the Missouri. In most sections the choice spots are along the banks, where you will find fish feeding on the surface during hatches and eating nymphs subsurface most of the rest of the time. But on this two-mile stretch you won't generally find that unless the water flows are very high. Then, fish move well away from the main current and hug the banks. Maybe it's the pressure they see from wading fisherman or possibly the subsurface structure, but they seem to have an aversion to the banks in 90% of this water.

This two-mile section is a good dry fly section during the

Baetis hatch in the spring and the Trico hatch in the summer. But it pales in comparison to other stretches of the river for those looking for top water action. It's not to say that fish here won't eat a caddis or a hopper, but it seems to take an almost blanket hatch to move them to the top except in spring and fall. The good news is that they love to feed subsurface on nymphs and streamers.

The Missouri has a strain of rainbow that is strong, healthy, and very willing to take a fly.

While floating, make certain to keep a little extra slack in your line. Dragging the fly, whether it's a nymph or dry, means you are destined to spend a long day watching others catch fish while you cast and change flies. These Missouri River trout do not like drag, even a little bit of drag. The whitefish, however, don't seem to mind. If you are catching nothing but "buglemouths," either there is too much drag or you're fishing the wrong habitat. In this section, the trout are generally found in the weedy areas and the whitefish in the weed-free ones. Whitefish are considered a game fish in Montana and if you get caught practicing "Squeeze and Release" on them, you may find yourself explaining your actions to a game warden.

Montana Department of Fish, Wildlife and Parks employs wardens that patrol the Missouri and other rivers, usually from the helm of 18-foot aluminum jet boats, but sometimes from land-based vehicles. Stay up-to-date on the fishing regulations, which are rewritten every two years for this Blue Ribbon trout stream. A copy of the regulations is available where licenses are sold or you can check the website at http://www.fwp.state.mt.us/

While nymphing this section, you will find that most of the takes will be very subtle, especially with small flies. The trout suck in the fly and then quickly expel it when they realize that it's not what they expected. Immediate response is needed here. If you wait for the indicator to completely submerge, you will miss most fish. The best nymph fishermen set the hook quickly when the indicator does anything out of the ordinary, and that often means just turning 90°. Oftentimes the flies will catch on the subsurface weeds or substrate, and that looks almost identical to strikes by fish. The only real way to know is to set the hook—if it pulls back it's probably a fish.

These weed beds can be very productive and make you want to spend the entire day there, but other anglers would enjoy the chance to catch a few also. River etiquette suggests that you catch a few and then move on. These are not the only pods you will find on this river, and fly fishing is not about numbers of fish caught.

An island about a mile downstream of the put-in on river right, is locally called the Bullpen. It got its name because the rancher often keeps several large bulls fenced in the area just upstream from it. A nice side channel runs between the island and the east shoreline. While it holds enough water to float through, a better strategy is to drop anchor on the island and wade fish the side channel. In low-water years, this is a favorite wading spot and is easy to get to from the small parking area, so you may want to pass if too many other anglers are there.

The best bet is to fish the weed beds from here to the Wolf Creek Bridge.

As you approach the bridge, keep an eye on the water just below the abutments, as they often are collection spots for hatching insects and trout. You will find another, heavily used, FAS on the east side of the river just below the bridge.

Across the river and a few hundred yards downstream is the mouth of Little Prickly Pear Creek. This small stream is the nursery for many Missouri River trout. Rainbows migrate up in the late winter or early spring, and browns move up in the fall. It is off limits to fishing during these spawning runs, but during the summer months you are free to fish it as long as you stay below the high water mark. Many fish often collect in the area just downstream of this feeder stream.

Beyond the creek, you are now in water more likely to produce pods of rising fish along the banks. The shoreline is often steeper and lined with overhanging willows and brush. If there is no hatch on, don't despair, as the nymphing will normally produce great results.

The shoreline on the west bank usually holds some great pods of fish. A few hundred yards below the mouth of the Little Prickly Pear is a small railroad bridge, and another few hundred yards below is another. This is a prime bank where you'll want to slow the boat down and fish hard.

A side channel on this west bank is navigable with moderate or higher flows and exits about a half-mile downstream. When the flows are sufficient this is a fun side channel, but when the flows are low it's little more than a stagnant pool. In this fairly narrow channel you will likely encounter wading fisherman who you won't see until you are sometimes right on them. Do your best to not put down their fish, but everyone should understand that there is little you can do to avoid infringing on their water in this tight space. An alternative is to anchor your boat and walk in.

If you continue floating the river's main stem, either bank is good. You will see a fairly large island on river right, and a smaller island in the middle of the river. The smaller island is called California Island, maybe because from the air it has that state's shape. Wading anglers cannot wade to California Island but can to the larger one. The side channel is floatable, but you might be running a gauntlet of fishermen, as it's shallow enough to wade during moderate and low flows. California Island is another hot spot, but be careful not to crowd others there before you. Either side and the tail of the island are good, and emerging hatches often collect at the tail making moves like NFL great Walter Payton to avoid the anxious trout. Nymphing is good here most of the time and wading around the island is easy in summer's normally low flows.

If you show up in the early morning just as the sun is hitting the island, you will often find large trout in the shallows exposing their dorsal fins as they forage for bait fish, spent wings left over from the night before, or early morning caddis and Tricos. Approach these ultra vulnerable and spooky fish with great caution and patience. If you do everything right you might have the opportunity to see one of these bad boys take your fly and explode in this shallow water as they head out to the main current. It's quite an amazing sight because when one spooks as he feels your hook, you'll see many others that you didn't know were there follow suit. Be prepared to run downstream as these explosive hits usually result in a panicked race toward the tail of the island, with you in hot pursuit as you watch more and more of your backing disappear into the water. Once the sun hits this shallow water, the fish slide back into the main current to avoid predators with long rods or sharp beaks.

As you look downstream from California Island, the river course remains fairly straight before it makes a turn to the right. Weed beds, mostly down the middle, hold trout, and the banks can hold sipping fish when a hatch is on. Just before the river turns, and during low flows, you will find a shallow gravel bar almost in the middle of the river. This is a good place to drop anchor and get out to work the area toward river left. You can't walk to shore from this gravel bar without swimming, so make sure your anchor is set well.

As you move around the bend you will see a very large island almost in the middle of the river, a side channel that flows down river left, and if the flows are low, you may even be able to see a small gravel bar to the right of the island. All of the area around the island fishes well with moderate flows, but if you float the side channel with low flows you will likely end up dragging your boat over some gravel. There is a high dirt bank on river right, and the slacker water next to the bank often finds fish sipping the hatch du jour as the insects get caught in the small back eddies.

Below the island is another gravel bar that is partially exposed in low-water years. This is another great place to drop anchor and wade fish. On river right is a side channel that goes around another island, but it's shallow on the bottom end, with flows below

4,000 cfs—and might leave you looking like the Lewis and Clark party as they pulled their dugouts on the Missouri 200 years ago.

You will probably find wading anglers on river right for the next couple of miles. The take-out at Craig is about two miles downstream and access is easy from the Rec Road on the east side of the river. The fishing here can be quite spectacular as the river braids and the shallows make for easy wading. Evening hatches of caddis seem to like this place and you will often find them struggling to adulthood chased by finned pursuers.

Horses and other livestock frequent the river at the mouth of Little Prickly Pear Creek. They are seldom a problem to wading anglers.

On river left is a series of rock weirs, courtesy of the local Trout Unlimited chapter. These partially submerged rocks slow the current and provide great habitat. In 1999 a guided fly fisher caught a 26" brown trout from this bank on a size #18 Lovebug.

These weirs give way to a riffle and then the river makes a sharp turn to the left. On the outside bend of this curve you will see a white bridge, and then steep banks that point down to a toilet bowl. This large back eddy collects huge numbers of struggling insects when a hatch is on, and fish will often percolate the water as they gorge themselves. It also collects everything else in the river from Styrofoam bait containers to aquatic grasses and branches. A high rock wall goes right down to the water guard-

ed by hundreds of mud swallows who inhabit it each year. Look for risers here as well as just downstream on river right, where a slow side channel diverts part of the river.

This channel goes under a low ranch bridge that looks remarkably like the flatbed railroad car it once was. If the water is too high at around 10,000 to 12,000 cfs, you won't be able to float under it. If the water is too low you'll have to drag your boat through. It's also a very popular wading spot so you may be pulling your raft through a bunch of irritated anglers. The fishing can be very good in this shallow side channel. If you find it unoccupied, beach your boat on the west side of the island and check it out.

On the main stem side of the island is good habitat for both nymphing and dry fly fishing and, across the Missouri on the left, is a deep back cut with a large rock outcropping at the bottom end. The locals, for good reason, call this the Bay of Pigs. The eddy downstream from the big rock also traditionally holds pods of slurping fish in the evenings or cloudy days.

As you pass the rock you'll see the Craig Bridge. The take-out is on river left just upstream of the bridge but, if you're up to it, fish are waiting for you before you quit for the day. There is a small but productive riffle in the middle of the river, with a side channel on river right. A riprap bank on the right, and often the tail of the last island on the left, also hold fish. Keep in mind that, if you miss the take-out, it will be very difficult to pull the boat back upstream on river left because of a sharp drop-off and steep riprap bank.

This is probably the craziest FAS on the river, and if you take out late there are probably a number of floaters eyeing the neon

An early morning launch at the Craig FAS. The Craig Bridge is a single-lane bridge built in the early 1900s. Time has taken its toll on this old boy and it will be replaced with new concrete and steel.

"Bar" sign that is only a long cast away. Load your boat and then move away so that others can load theirs. In summer there are often children from the adjacent campground with dogs and little brothers in tow who are anxious to know how your day went. Local stray dogs will follow you around because people in waders have given them their leftover lunches for years. It can be hectic, but take the time to relive the highlights of the day with your friends.

Craig to Mid-Cañon

8 MILES–SEE MAP PAGE 30

As you leave the boat ramp be prepared to start fishing right away. The bank on river left is normally very productive as well as the riffle, known as the Craig Riffle, that is just below the bridge in the middle of the river. As the river bends slightly to the right there are numerous nymphing opportunities in the weed beds that grow in the middle of the river, but during the Trico hatches of summer, look to the edges of the river for huge pods of sipping rainbows.

Campgrounds, like this one adjacent to the Craig FAS, offer a ringside seat to the action on the river. Many anglers will launch their boats and then anchor on a shallow gravel bar to rig their rods or catch some fish!

Many people mistake them for small riffles the first time through. They will surface for other hatches but they seem more stimulated by the massive Trico hatches of July and August.

As the river makes a slight bend to the left, you will see a high bank just upstream of a large rock. This is called Jackson's Rock, and the back eddy below this rock is a thing of beauty. Most days it's a bit of a toilet bowl, with massive amounts of insects in various stages of life clinging to free-drifting grasses and whatever else the river delivers to this eddy. Consequently, trout gather here in large numbers to gorge. When it all comes together it's an amazing sight–hundreds of rising fish making an audible slurping sound if you can get your buddies to shut up for

a moment. The hardest part of this hole is getting the fish to see your fly with the thousands of naturals on the water. Also, with all the garbage swirling around, your drifts will be short before you hook the flotsam or fish. These fish will spook and go down but, when they are in full attack mode, nothing short of a Tomahawk missile is going to keep them down. The more they are spooked and put down, the longer it takes for them to come back up. This is another one of those honey holes where you want to catch a few and then move on. If you see boats of guys upstream anchored and drinking coffee, know that they are not admiring your casting prowess, but rather they are waiting their turn at the watering hole.

Downstream is a shallow, mid-river run that will often hold rising fish. This run is also very weedy, so it nymphs well, but you'll have to shorten the distance between indicator and flies. As the river turns to the left, it braids, revealing several islands, gravel bars, and channels in low-water years. This part of the river is different after high water as are many river environs. The main channel bisects the islands. Except for the channel on extreme river right, all this water fishes well and is a great place to beach the boat and wade fish.

If you just like to cover water, hug the bank on river right below the islands all the way down to the Interstate bridge (**1**).

Islands dot the river between Craig and Mid-Cañon. Many of them are only accessible to floaters, especially during higher water flows.

A few hundred yards upstream of the Interstate bridge, watch the slickwater downstream of the rock outcroppings for sipping fish. The bridge columns break the current for the fish, so they will pod up below there when food is available.

A small island is on river right just below the bridge. The side channel is fished better afoot than afloat; it is narrow and shallow but tends to be productive. On river left is more of Trout Unlimited's handiwork, signs of restoration with some sprouting willows. In this semi-arid climate, riparian restoration can take decades.

River left then has a high bank going up to the railroad tracks. You'll see a very high cliff that drops down to the water and a very deep hole. In spring, Canada geese nest on these cliffs—you can sometimes see their offspring making their first flights. Surprisingly, they all seem to make it safely to the water, although some of them have the grace of an NFL nose-tackle on roller skates.

On river right is another nice island that is home to a series of weed beds and a shallow side channel that seems to have activity even in the lowest of water years. It's always a treat to catch a 20"-plus brown out of 10" of water in the middle of a sunny day at the end of the Trico hatch. If the fish seem to be slow to rise, tie on a Parachute Hopper and drift it over their heads. Often you'll find a fish or two in the mood for dessert. You'll likely have to make a long and accurate cast.

Below the big cliff, river left has a great sheltered bank where the water flows under overhanging willows. You'll regularly find bank cruisers looking up for the clumsy flies to lose their grip on the branches or leaves and fall helplessly into the water. There are numerous rock outcrops and large boulders here, and it drops off quickly from the bank to deep water. A great sub-surface structure here offers a near-perfect habitat for the fish. The current is slowed by the structure and the foliage along the bank is a resting place for different hatches. It all adds up to great water.

When the water shallows, if you look across to river right, you will see a campground and boat ramp. This is Stickney Creek. The side channel between the island and the take-out is a really sweet spot, but more often than not many people from the campground noticed the rising fish as they relaxed by a campfire the night before. There is plenty of water to float, but if the channel is occupied you may want to stick to the main channel and target the tail of the island or the other islands that dot the river for the next mile.

River right has you literally fishing in residents' backyards, and river left has a fairly high riprap bank that ends at another high cliff—all good water. Directly across the river on the east side is another take-out. This one is called Spite Hill. It doesn't look like much, with no defined concrete ramp to tip you off. It is a small campground, often lined with campers and bank fisherman because you can drive a vehicle right to the water's edge. Sometimes getting your boat out means asking someone to move their car or lawn chair first.

Downstream on river left you'll find the Tractor Hole. Unless the river is at flood stage, you'll see a very old farm tractor on the bank. It's just one of many abandoned farm implements along this bank, which you may or may not see depending on the flow. Keep in mind that some are still very sharp and, as one fellow guide found out, can rip a hole in the hull of an aluminum boat. For the fish, it is like a McDonald's playground with all sorts of hiding places.

The riprap bank on river right is perfect for summertime Hopper-Dropper rigs. A fairly shallow but productive riffle runs mid-river. It is about a half-mile above the next take-out on the right, which is Dearborn. You'll see the Dearborn River flowing into the Missouri on the left and the Interstate bridge (**2**) above you.

If you have driven here on the Recreation Road, you'll likely miss Dearborn Fishing Access Site the first time because there is no campground. Unless other rigs are parked here, you might drive past because this steep ramp is hard to see from the road. The landmarks are the bridge and the Dearborn River coming into the Missouri on river left.

The next take-out is Mid-Cañon, and it's about 1.5 miles downstream on river left.

As you pass under the bridge, a high cliff on river right looks promising, but a better bet is river left; it's shallower, has less current, and typically is a conveyer belt for floating insects. A series of weirs in front of several houses on the right holds fish for the next half mile or so, but the bank on the left is also productive.

One really great part of fishing the Missouri is that in so many places on the river it really doesn't matter if you fish right or left. There are so many fish per mile that if you come around a bend and find someone already fishing the bank you were heading for, you can simply move to the other side of the river and have a good time. Rivers are in a constant state of change and where the fish are holding during high-water years is often not where they are in low water years. But if you consider what fish need it will better lead you to them. They need food, oxygen, protection from predators, and a current that won't deplete their strength. Once you know the river and understand the structure, hatches, and trout habits, it will be hard to have a bad day.

From the Interstate bridge (**2**) to the take-out is such a place where the fishing is normally good on both banks. This is just a fun river to float. You don't have to row your ass off all day long in order to keep yourself out of harm's way. Instead, the rower can often kick back and enjoy the view of the various critters that inhabit the river and its shoreline. It's amazing how often you will see an osprey dive and catch a fish, then watch a bald eagle bombard the osprey until the smaller raptor drops the meal that the eagle recovers.

Just upstream of the Mid Canon take out on river left is a Lewis and Clark camping site. The river braids again into numerous islands and gravel bars. The take out is almost even with the downstream side of these islands, and which channel

51

Some boat launches, like this one at Mid-Cañon, are little more than a small area cleared of willows and brush. Many years ago this was the site of a ferry crossing.

you take isn't important if you don't mind pulling your boat back upstream. Fishing is good in all these channels—but if you take the channel on the extreme river right, you are going to struggle to make the ramp that is on the other side of the river.

Mid-Cañon is another campground and, if you've driven here for the first time, it may be a bit confusing how to get back to the Interstate. Simply follow the dirt road that goes north out of the campground. Turn left to cross the railroad tracks, and then turn right. The Interstate will be right in front of you. In case you are turned around, Craig and Helena are south and Great Falls and Cascade are north.

Mid-Cañon to Mountain Palace

6 MILES—SEE MAP PAGE 31

With the exception of July and August, Mid-Cañon is not a heavily used Fishing Access Site, and the campground isn't usually crowded, but because of the shallow water and islands, it tends to collect an above-average number of wading anglers. Sometimes your first task after launching your boat is to avoid running through their water.

The far bank of river right is productive, steep, and normally free of competition. This high riprap bank is home to a pod of resident rainbows, but unless there is a Trico hatch on, they will most likely eat subsurface nymphs early in the morning. At certain times of the year, namely July and early August, you can launch late morning and see some pale morning duns coming off here. But generally, subsurface flies will work best—especially in the early morning.

The first of three Interstate bridges (**3**) is visible even from the put-in. On river left is a nice run that ends at a steep cliff— the small back eddies along the rock wall hold fish that will often show their presence by breaking the surface and sipping the hatch. This can be great streamer water, and Woolly Buggers of brown, black, and especially olive often bring the larger 'bows and browns out of their slumber.

Below the cliff there is a high riprap bank with the railroad tracks just above it. Downstream a couple of miles are two islands. If you float to the far right and the flows are very low, you will float through a small amount of whitewater more like a kiddy rollercoaster ride than anything serious. But, if you happen to go through the white water sideways while you're high fivin' each other about the fish you just released, you might end up bailing water out of your boat.

Just to the left, you'll see a shallow that is exposed when flows are below about 3,500 cfs. If the flows are higher, be careful to hit it bow first, or avoid it altogether. You can also float between the two islands, and this is probably the safest route. The current speed increases here as the Missouri narrows, but it's really not much of a challenge to an intermediate rower.

The far left channel holds a couple of really large boulders toward the bottom end and it gets pretty shallow during low water flows. You may not be able to see wading anglers fishing at the bottom of the first of two islands as you enter this channel.

The left bank is high, steep, and rocky—perfect shelter for fish. The current runs toward this bank, depositing food that is floating free in the drift. The bank continues almost all the way to the next Interstate bridge (**4**). Below the bridge the river makes a turn to the left, but the main current runs adjacent to the somewhat steep right bank. It's a good bank to fish, but its rocks extend well into the water and—with the added current—it's a bad place to drop an anchor. If you need to stop, pull to the other side of the river. This current

Many of the high banks in this section have large rocks underwater from when the old highway was built. These structures are good habitat for the fish.

is deceptively fast, especially in moderate flows, and the large rocks on the substrate will wedge an anchor in an instant. Then, if you don't swamp your boat, you're going to have a hell of a time retrieving your anchor. The water is too deep and fast to wade and you won't easily row upstream of your anchor.

If you happen upon a hot, breezy afternoon you might try casting a Hopper-Dropper rig on the other bank, which is lined with a few houses and large willow trees. On river right you'll see two large rock outcroppings with riprap that look very much like what you encountered just after you launched at Mid-Cañon. We call this déjà vu. The fishing is also identical to that sweet little spot upstream.

This is the last Interstate bridge (**5**), (the Gary Cooper Bridge) you will encounter on this stretch and you may notice that the river is starting to look more and more like a freestone river. By fall the aquatic weeds will be at their full growth, and if you happen to be here after a heavy freeze you might think you are fish-

The river twists and turns in the canyon section, and the high walls overlooking the river are home to many birds and other wildlife.

Just below the Interstate bridge and above an island on river left is a large back eddy and deep hole. This is sometimes a bit of a toilet bowl, but often holds trout anxious to eat a dry fly. The hole is too deep to nymph productively, but you can often get strikes by dropping a nymph off your dry fly.

Bank left is great. More riprap and, often, the risers are within inches of the rocks. The river bends to the right and this is the outside of that bend. Another high wall and the riprap bank continue below it. This high wall is a favorite diving platform for some of the local kids who live across the river. When you see how high

ing on a golf course. Grass that has died and broken off from the bottom is now free-floating in the river. These huge green barges are at the whim of the wind and current as they momentarily put down pods of rising fish on their downstream journey. If you happen to be wade fishing and get caught in their path, you'll realize their tremendous force. But, when these "golf course fairways" get caught on the rocks along the banks and float into back eddies, they provide great shelter and, sometimes, food for the fish. Casting a hopper or an attractor like a Royal Double Wing and drifting it within inches of these floating weed mats will often solicit a response from a hiding trout. In low-water years, these weed mats can show up in early summer and stay all season long. Spring runoffs usually generate enough push to move them out to the Montana plains and high winds can often send them sailing.

the wall is, you'll realize how deep the water is just below it.

Watch for the side channel on river left that flows around Goose Shit Island. If you take a break or wade fish from this island in the spring when the Canada geese are nesting, you'll know how it got its name. The side channel has enough water to float except during very low flows, but it's best to beach your boat and fish both sides of the island. I estimate this island to be a bit over halfway in this six-mile float.

The bank along river right is shallow but good, but notice that there is more exposed structure now. The leisurely pace of the river is changing as the elevation drops a little faster and the current speeds up in places.

While either bank is equally productive from here to the take-out at Mountain Palace, if you find yourself on this part of the river in late afternoon and want to try something different than nymphing, try a hopper or other terrestrial. Casting a Foam Beetle against the banks with a good reach cast (*see* Seasons of the Missouri: Winter) can solicit some interesting responses on those hot summer afternoons. Some of the takes will be very subtle and others will have you thinking that someone dropped a cinder block out of an airplane and it landed on your fly! Large flies sometimes get large responses from large fish.

When you notice that the Interstate is moving away from the river and the Recreation Road, you are about a mile from the take-out. You might notice a small, undesignated put-in on river right. The local guides call this Grassy Bank. This area is great trout water. In July, if you float through it late in the day, you can be rewarded with tremendous caddis hatches, normally just before sunset. You often hear the fish splashing long after dark. If you don't know the river very well, and it's dark, it will be easy to miss the Mountain Palace take-out on river right. It's somewhat hidden in a side channel next to a large island. If you pass it by floating down the main course of the river, the only indication of your error may be the few campfires at the campground. One landmark is the Fly Fisherman's Inn on the right. It's across the Rec road and up the hill and visible from the river during daylight hours.

Mountain Palace to Pelican Point
6 MILES–SEE MAP PAGE 32

Before you launch your boat here, be aware of a series of rapids on this section of the Missouri River. While none is life

The numerous houses that dot the river are clustered in areas like this one near Mid-Cañon FAS.
Without a boat you would have to walk a lot of shoreline to reach this section of the river.

55

The river at Mountain Palace runs very narrow and deep with a sheer rock face on one side.
The fish will come up from the depths for hatches. The channel quickly widens after this point.

threatening to an accomplished rower, this wouldn't be the water you'd want to row if this were your first day on the oars. In low water you could do a lot of hull damage to a drift boat, and in the right circumstances you could even capsize or swamp a boat. Much depends on the river's flow, how much your boat sits down in the water, and your experience level. The white water is only about three-fourths of a mile long, and begins under the Interstate bridge near Hardy Creek.

Immediately across from the Mountain Palace FAS is an island. When the hatch is in full swing, you're likely to see pods of rising fish off the tail of this island and following the current down to where it runs along the right bank. Wade fishing this side channel, or the river side of the island, can be productive–either nymphing or top water fly fishing, depending on time of day and what insects are active.

A large, steep rock face goes down to the river on the right, at one of the deepest parts of the river. During summer months, kids soar from this natural diving rock, but if you launch in early morning you're likely to miss watching those future Olympians.

Downstream of these rocks you face two choices. River right is shallow with a soft dirt shore vegetation that often gives up those fish looking to eat what falls off the bank. River left sweeps to the right, along a riprap bank lined with willows all the way down to the Hardy ("Untouchables" from its one-time movie

The "Untouchables" Bridge was the backdrop of a movie with Sean Connery and Kevin Costner. Now it is just a way across to the Recreation Road and an interesting sight for fly fishers.

role) Bridge, where the Recreation Road crosses the Missouri for the last time.

From the bridge downstream, you'll find a fairly shallow stretch that fish move into when the hatch is on—and out of when it's over. River right has a small branch of the main current running close to the bank, and river left runs under some willows and then into a back eddy. This is all prime water. If the weather is hot and you are hitting this stretch in late morning or early afternoon, it's great hopper and attractor water. If you're here during a Trico or PMD hatch, you'll be rewarded with lots of targets to cast your flies to. If there are no visibly rising fish, a

The terrain changes rapidly after it exits the canyon near the Hardy Interstate bridge. This area, near Pelican Point, is lovely in its own right.

hopper and nymph dropper rig can produce, and a two-fly Nymph rig with an indicator can work well also.

On river left you'll see a campground and a boat ramp. This is Prewett Creek. If you take out here and decide to pull your boat from the gravel portion instead of the concrete ramp, be careful, especially if you don't have a four-wheel drive vehicle. The gravel can be very loose and, with the sharp angle to the water, it's easy to spin wheels and dig holes without ever moving away from the water. This FAS is much smaller than most and there is little parking. If you park in a camping spot you'll likely be fined unless you fill out a camping permit and pay for that spot. The area right in front of the boat ramp can get very congested with kids, adults, and pets—as well as vehicles.

Across from the boat ramp you'll see some of the most vertical rock walls on the Missouri River. This spectacular area is home to eagles, mountain goats, and all sorts of other creatures. It marks the end of the canyon and the beginning of the plains. The river, no longer contained by rock, stretches out. All along this very steep wall are receptive fish. While nymphing can produce numbers of trout, the fish in this section seem to have an affinity for floating morsels, especially during terrestrial days. Those are days where there is enough wind to blow beetles, hoppers, and ants off their perches on the water's edge and enough sun and warmth to pull them from their hiding places in search of food and companionship.

As you leave the canyon you'll see the last Interstate bridge (**6**) from here to Cascade. The very large protruding boulders on river left are home to lots of hungry trout, but don't get so distracted that you miss the white water that begins right under the bridge. The first set is just a warm-up, so you may think that the term "rapids" was misused here. Then, as the river bends to the left, you'll see what looks like more broken water but nothing to worry about. The river current is going to pull you aggressively toward the left bank and, without some fervent back rowing, you may find yourself banging the rocks. You'll get a very brief rest, but the biggest challenge is yet to come. The river widens considerably now and, downstream, you'll see a

*Summer afternoon thunderstoms can come up quickly and leave just as quickly. The result is a refreshing drop in
temperature which can be a relief from the heat. From the Pelican Point FAS you can watch the storm move away.*

very shallow rocky or riffled portion, depending on the flow. This is Halfbreed Rapids. During very low flows there is a lot of exposed rock in the middle of the river. The main current splits here—one stem toward the right bank and one toward the left. To the left is deeper, but there is little room for error. To the right is less large structure, but if you hit it sideways it's a real hull bang. Whichever way you choose, it will pay to be watchful.

Cottonwoods line the river near the town of Cascade as the river slowly winds through ranch land and prairie.

During certain flows, and with an experienced rower, this can be a lot of fun. If this is your first time through and you don't have a lot of time in the rower's seat, remember to control the boat by back rowing and steering with the stern. You may get into shallow water where you won't be able to drop the oar very far. Keep in mind that if you hook an oar it can turn your boat sharply and take you out of position in a blink of an eye. At times, an experienced rower will get through this section and ask what the big fuss is about. For the novice, going through for the first time, it might be quite nerve-wracking.

Below the rapids the river becomes mostly tranquil. There are a few riffles but really nothing much of a challenge. In mid-summer this is hopper heaven. The larger brown trout seem to have an affinity for these large, leggy terrestrials. Cast them to the banks especially where you see the abrupt drop-offs. During banner grasshopper years, the grass and willows along the banks sing to you with the insects' monotonous voices. When the wind blows, many hoppers find their way into the river. The trout are well conditioned to these large pieces of wiggling protein.

Of course if there is a hatch on, this last 2.5 miles to the take-out will display noses sipping or slurping caddis or mayflies but, generally, throughout the summer you will have to hit this section late in the day to see the caddis hatches. Nymphing or stripping a streamer is a good mainstay for those days when they snub your best hopper imitations and there is no visible hatch.

For the most part stick to the banks. This substrate is less weedy overall than it was upstream by Holter Dam, or at least it's a different kind of aquatic fauna. Small gravel bars are exposed during very low flows, but for the most part this is a floating section rather than a wading section. If you see a pod of fish, and want to work it by wading, there are many places shallow enough to do so. River left has a fairly high bank for most of this course, even when you get almost to the take-out and the river braids through several islands. River right is flatter and more conducive to wade fishing.

When the river braids, you are almost to the take-out. There are about six islands here, and the fishing is good around all of them. If you stay to the far left, it will take you down a side channel that winds around, empties back into the mainstem, and takes you very close to the take-out ramp. These islands offer an easy place to drop anchor, and the channels are very easy to wade. River right also has a nice side channel, but it's much tougher to wade fish through the upper part. Both offer good fishing opportunities.

As you pass the tail of the islands, look to the left. This takeout is on a peninsula of sorts. This marks Pelican Point. From the upstream side, you'll see the familiar FAS outhouse and, often, parked cars. The boat ramp is on the downstream side, tucked back into a small cove that is somewhat concealed, especially from upstream and when it's empty. The next take-out is 8.5 miles downriver.

Before you get out of your boat, notice that the river bottom drops off very sharply. If you pull your boat in and drop the anchor on the sand, the water under the bow is going to be over the bow angler's head. Unless he's tired of being dry and warm, you might caution him to exit the stern of the boat. After loading your boat from this very steep ramp, drive to the end of the dirt road and turn left on the paved Rec Road to get to the Interstate.

Nola Krahe skillfully works the nymph patterns she tied last winter. Good approach techniques and good drag-free presentations are the key to successful angling on the "Mo."

Pelican Point to Cascade

8.5 MILES—SEE MAP PAGE 33

If you arrive at the FAS here at Pelican Point, and those very large cottonwood trees are waving and dancing in the wind like a Super Bowl cheering section, you might want to reconsider, especially if the wind is out of the north. This piece of the Missouri River is well out of the protection of the canyon, and when wind blows down here, little can slow it. The other down side is that, once you put in, there is no take-out for 8.5 miles. I have put in here and changed my mind well over a mile downstream—when we decided that it was easier to row upstream with the wind rather than downstream with the current. If you decide to brave it anyway on days like these, you probably won't be able to fish much, but you will be able to tell your friends about the day that you had white caps on the water in your boat. If you start floating this section and you are all by yourself, you might wonder if you are the smartest person in the world, or if everyone else had checked the weather forecast while you didn't.

The river slows in this section, so you need to adjust your downriver pace, especially during low flows. If you take too many breaks or stop too often to wade fish, you may not see the lights of Cascade until well after most of the townsfolk have gone to bed. There is often very good fishing down here, but you'll likely notice that the average size of fish is smaller than upstream. This part of the river sees more spawning trout as more make their redds here in the river's mainstem rather than venturing up into the tributaries. Gravel beds and small riffles dot this section, making for much better spawning habitat, as well as a nursery for fry and fingerlings. The result is that adolescents are mixed in with older trout, and, while this happens upstream, it's the norm here.

Thankfully the wind doesn't blow 40 mph every day, so this section can be lots of fun. On many days it seems like you could spend the entire day just downstream of the put-in on river right, or on river left, or in the weed beds in the middle of the river. But then you would miss all the great water between here and the Cascade Bridge!

You can see an island from the launch site, and this is often a great place to stop and wade fish to get your bearings. The river looks and acts much like a freestone river here. It has lost its tail-water look and flow, and replaced it with the more typical structure of riffles, runs, and pools. It's also shallower and wider.

Look for pods of rising fish along the banks and back eddies, keeping in mind you might be looking at fingerlings, locally known as dinks. In this situation, a good pair of binoculars can be more valuable than that new four-piece 6-weight rod you just bought.

About 1.5 miles downstream, after a long riprap bank on river left, you will find where the river dives into an abrupt bank. This is called the Pump Hole because of the very large water pump that is visible. The Recreation Road is fairly close to the river here, making it one of the few places where you could easily get out and thumb a ride if you got into trouble. It isn't a place to get your boat out, as the road is still about 50 yards up a fairly steep bank. It is, however, a pretty good hole both here and around the corner in the long run that comes off the corner.

This entire 8.5-mile stretch of river is one of the few places on the river where you can find stonefly hatches with any consistency. During those hot days of July and August, this is where you'll want to dig out those attractor and terrestrial patterns. Some days the sound of the locusts is almost deafening.

Most of this section seems to be somewhat characterless compared to the canyon portion. You have to invest the time to see the true beauty of it. You'll find riffles running under very large cottonwood trees and most of the banks down here are high and made of dirt. Basically, you'll want to fish the banks and the riffles, especially when the water temperatures of summer gets into the mid- or even high 60s. The coolest water will be under the overhanging trees or brush, and the highest oxygen levels will be in the riffled water. Since the river is very wide, most of the trout food is near river's edge. The exceptions are the braided islands.

About three miles into this float you'll see a ranch house on river right and a steep riprap bank. A large pile of rock is submerged about 20 feet from shore. If the flow is fairly low, it's possible to drop an anchor on this rock pile. Around the pile is a very deep hole, which is great Wooly Bugger water, and along the bank you'll often find fish awaiting your dry flies.

The river braids a lot after this point, forming numerous islands and side channels. The flow out of Holter Dam will decide whether they run enough water to float a drift boat through. Many of these side channels offer some of the very best fishing opportunities. It is like fishing a small stream if you decide to get out and wade fish. But keep in mind that when you are here, you are only about halfway to the take-out.

You'll see the Interstate at a distance a few times more before you start seeing a lot of houses on river left. At this point you are adjacent to the town of Cascade, but still with more than two miles to go to the take-out at the Cascade Bridge.

Nymphing can be very effective, but since this is mostly shallow water, dry flies or streamers on a floating line are your best bet. As you near the bridge, you'll see a high dirt bank on river right lined with cottonwood trees, with a large island on your left. You should be able to see cars, or headlights, where the road crosses the river there. The take-out is under the bridge on river right.

The Cascade Bridge marks the end of this float.

To return to the Interstate, turn right onto the bridge and into Cascade. Continue two blocks to a stop sign. Turn left and then follow the signs to the Interstate if you are going south to Craig or Helena, or turn right at the stop sign and follow the signs to the Interstate to go north to Great Falls.

While there are trout to be caught downstream from Cascade, it's not water that is readily accessible either by drift boat or by car. The next take-out is miles away at the town of Ulm. People mostly fish this water from jet boats for warm water species.

Hatches on the river can be very intense and they rarely go unnoticed by the fish.

Hatches, Presentation, and Patterns

Once, while guiding a man and his wife, I noticed that the woman kept swatting at the *Baetis* (mayflies) that landed on her shirt and vest. She told her husband that she wanted to quit because the insects were biting her. The exchange between her and myself went like this:

"They can't bite you."

"Why?"

"Because they have no mouthparts that can bite or sting."

"That's ridiculous, how do they eat?"

"They don't eat."

"Really?"

"Honest."

She then quit swatting and started catching some fish undisturbed by the mating swarms that were forming just ahead of the boat. I told her the *Baetis* were involved in a massive sexual orgy, but they were not interested in food. She smiled and nodded.

Studying insects may not be something that you devote a lot of time to but knowing at least the fundamentals of aquatic entomology will greatly help you identify what trout are eating at any given time. Knowing the behavior of these insects will allow you to catch fish while others around you are dividing their time between scratching their heads and changing flies.

Science classifies things in nature to better study them. For example, there are many different kinds of birds: insect eaters, seed eaters, predatory flesh eaters, and those that eat carrion. If you are driving down the road and a voice from the backseat asks, "Is that a robin eating that dead skunk?" you would know that it wasn't a robin because they don't eat carrion. If you went home and dusted off that bird book you bought long ago, you would have somewhere to begin. You observed the size and color of the bird, what it was eating, and maybe some other features. When you find a photo that looks like what you saw you could then identify it from the description of the animal, its habitat, and other characteristics. The same is true for aquatic insects.

Many orders of aquatic insects are of interest to the fly fisherman. On the Missouri there are three that dominate and one lesser—mayflies (Ephemeroptera), caddisflies (Trichoptera), true flies (Diptera) and stoneflies (Plecoptera).

I must admit a certain fascination with aquatic insects. While it's true that if trout didn't eat them I probably would pay them little attention, they are a very interesting life form that fossil records show have been around for over 250 million years. Trout, on the other hand, have only been around about 70 or 80 million years. Mayflies are an integral part of fly fishing history.

Perhaps it was their upright wings that caught the attention of early anglers, or maybe it was the whispering clouds of mating swarms. Either way, these delicate insects are etched into our sport as much as Vince Lombardi is etched into football. Their vulnerability to water pollution makes them the proverbial canary in the coal mine, and many species have become extinct on eastern United States streams.

Mayflies (Ephemeroptera)

LARVA: If you kick over a river rock and find a small larva (nymph), how do you determine if it's a mayfly? There are several obvious clues. If it has three tails, it's a mayfly. Caddis and midges have no tails, and stoneflies have two tails. Some mayflies have two tails and, while you would know this larva wasn't a

Early morning Tricos quickly move into mating swarms. The swarms are so intense they look like columns of smoke or dust. Soon billions of these tiny mayflies will die and cover the water.

caddis or midge, you could look at the end of its legs with a magnifier to see if it has a claw. If there is no claw, it's most likely a stonefly, as most mayflies have a single claw. Mayfly larva also have well developed eyes. There are of course many other distinguishing characteristics, but these are easy identifying features.

ADULT: Mayflies do not pupate like caddis or midges. Instead, when mature, they float or swim to or just under the surface film. There, the exoskeleton nymphal shuck is cracked down the back, and the sub-imago (dun) crawls out, dries its wings, and flies off.

Its wings are milky at this stage and it cannot reproduce until it sheds this layer to reveal a newly transparent wing and a richer body color. No other insect has these two winged stages. In this adult stage, mayflies can be distinguished from other Orders by their upright wings, which adult caddis, midges, and stoneflies do not have. While at rest, the dun wings are smoky-opaque as well as upright. Most mayflies have two pairs of wings, but often the hind wings are nothing more than small stubs, and so not easily seen.

Just what triggers these hordes of bottom-living nymphs to leave their water homes and head for their reproduction stage isn't exactly known, but most guesses include water temperature and length of daylight. The duns quickly molt, revealing transparent wings and more distinct body color. These adults, or spinners, are now ready to reproduce. They have no digestive system now and must mate before they die so they head out to find the mating swarms where the males fly up and down and the females fly through the swarm. Mating takes place in flight and the well-developed eyes of the males come in handy in identifying females. Females then deposit the eggs. Some species fly above the water and drop the eggs, some lay the eggs directly on the water either by landing on the surface or touching the water surface with their abdomens, and some dive into the water to deposit them directly on the substrate. The females that deposit on the surface generally die immediately afterward and their wings will appear to resemble airplane wings as they are now no longer upright but instead are 90° to the abdomen. This is generally referred to as a spent spinner and when it happens en masse it's called the spinner fall.

The Missouri River has three major mayfly hatches and some other smaller ones. They are Bluewinged Olives (*Baetis*), Pale Morning Duns (*Ephemerella infrequens, E. inermis*) and Tricos (*Tricorythodes minutus*).

Bluewinged Olives *(Baetis)*

Also known as BWOs, these small and delicate mayflies are normally the first hatch of the year other than midges and we first start seeing them in April. Their hatch usually lasts only a few weeks. Another species hatches in July, and the third and smallest species—referred to as Pseudos (*Pseudocloeon*)—starts in mid-September and often lasts into early November.

LARVA: These small nymphs are very mottled, including their three tails. The abdomen is highly segmented and lined with gills, but slender. Wingpads, especially on nearly mature nymphs, are very obvious. The best imitations are Pheasant Tails, RS-2s, Lovebug, Lightning Bug, and Hit and Run nymphs in size #16 and #18, dead-drifted on or very near the bottom. Always be alert for a take on the swing. Beadhead versions of all these patterns seem to have more productivity than those without beads.

EMERGERS: BWOs seem to spend a lot of time struggling either just below or on top of the surface film. They are very fast swimmers as nymphs, and then seem almost frantic after leaving the safety of the bottom. It might be because the hatch often occurs during rainy or even snowy days, and the higher humidity means it will take longer to dry their wings. The trout prey on them heavily during this stage. A soft light drizzle or snow is your best friend during a blue wing hatch on the Missouri. There have been many times when guys are smiling with chattering teeth. Dress warm, especially during the spring and fall hatches, and be prepared for a treat. Fish the same patterns as the nymphs but without beadheads for the emergers, and drop them off the patterns for the duns.

DUNS: As the nymphal shuck opens, the head, legs, and wings emerge while the duns float wherever the river's current takes them. They somehow lose their center tail from the larva stage, and now have only two tails. They are easy pickin's for the trout, and they know it. The takes are often soft and without fanfare but methodical. Often you can count the seconds of the trout's feeding rhythm and it will repeat over and over until he's hooked

or spooked. The best patterns are a BWO Cripple, BWO Emerger, Hi-Vis Parachute, or an Adams in sizes #16 and #18.

ADULT: Fish the same dry patterns as the dun stage. I rarely see a major BWO spinner fall on the Missouri and consequently don't fish it much, but when I have, a Clear Wing Spinner in a size #16 or #18 worked fine.

Pale Morning Duns
(Ephemerella infrequens, E. inermis)

PMD hatches usually show up by mid-July and last until mid-September. They are easy to spot as the adults are large compared to other upwing insects on the Missouri, and they are light yellow in color with almost-white wings. Many of my clients, as well as students in my fly-tying classes, tell me that this is the most frustrating hatch of all. Thousands of very visible flies on the water with fish taking them—and even the most elaborate quill wing patterns are snubbed, often leaving the angler heading for the nearest watering hole to dull his pain and humiliation with adult beverages.

In sampling rivers with a seine I have found that an inordinate amount of PMDs never make it to adulthood. A good 30% are somehow crippled, stillborn, or stuck in the nymphal shuck, unable to get

Mayflies are common on the Missouri and these Baetis *adults are ready for mating.*

free, and I'm at a loss to explain why such a high percentage never make it to maturity. Trout are predators, and these finned wolves will focus on the weak and infirm—your choice of patterns should reflect this behavior. The high-riding quill-wing adult patterns work well when the PMDs first start showing up on the river. But after even a few days, the trout basically ignore them. So most of the time when you see active feeding during a PMD hatch, you are probably seeing the trout take those insects that for some reason get stuck trying to escape the nymphal shuck. The fish will routinely ignore your patterns closely resembling the healthy adults that fly off.

Trico adult just after molting.

LARVA: These nymphs are crawlers and have three tails. They generally are a bit stouter and larger than the *Baetis* nymphs, although they also are somewhat mottled, especially on their legs and tails. Their coloring is usually in the brown and olive tones. Again, the beadhead Pheasant Tail, Lovebug, RS-2, Lightning Bug, and Hit and Run work well in sizes #14 to #18. Fish them dead-drifted on or near the bottom under a strike indicator.

EMERGER: This is the most productive stage of the hatch. Since PMDs are not swimmers, they migrate to the surface in a very clumsy manner—often getting picked off by waiting trout like bad guys in a Nintendo game. Often the nymphs will crawl to slower water to emerge, and the trout will follow. The first PMDs of the day will usually overlap the morning Trico hatch and start coming off mid-day. Combining the two patterns with a two-fly

rig will usually tell you which hatch the fish are keying on. I like to tie a PMD Cripple pattern on as the top fly during the Trico hatch because it's easier to see and the fish often hit it instead of the smaller Trico that I drop as a trailer. Dead drift a PMD Cripple or a PMD Emerger in sizes #14 to #18 through the pods of rising fish. If they are still a little tentative, drop a one-size-smaller Lovebug, Pheasant Tail Nymph, or Pheasant Tail Soft Hackle off the dry fly pattern.

ADULT: Except for rare times, the adult patterns are not the most effective ways to get fish to strike PMDs. Experiment—and if you find patterns that consistently catch trout, I would love to hear about them. I've got boxes of high-riding PMD adult patterns that caught only occasional fish.

Tricos *(Tricorythodes)*

Tricos can make you go blind if you keep playing with them. While you might occasionally see a natural Trico that could be matched with a #18, most effective patterns are in the #22 and #24 range. Looking into the rising sun and trying to figure out which speck of white lint is your pattern is tough duty. The best way to handle the situation for this and any other small dry fly pattern is to tie on a larger fly and drop the smaller one off of it. Then you are using the large pattern as a strike indicator and you won't have to make all those trips to the ophthalmologist.

Tricos are the smallest mayfly on the Missouri, but the fish will key on them so consistently each morning that you can almost set your watch by it. The bad news is that if you are a late sleeper you might not even know this hatch exists. Often on hot summer days it starts at 6 or 7 a.m. and it's all over by 10 or 11. If the wind comes up, the hatch may not even last that long—if it happens at all. The trout garbage feed on these small insects— they stay near the surface and scoop them up like blue whales eating plankton, often eating several at one time. Because the fish hold so close to the surface your approach needs to be stealthy and quiet so as not to send them scattering. Your presentation also needs to include a lot of finesse. Catching the large Missouri River rainbows, many of them over 18", on a size #22 dry fly is worth that hour or two of sleep you sacrificed to the fish gods.

The hatches normally start to occur in mid-July and continue until the first part of September. As an adult, this is a very short-lived insect. The hatch often will begin before the morning sun hits the water. The duns will molt immediately after they emerge, then you will see enormous mating swarms along the banks as early as 7 or 8 a.m. The females drop the fertilized eggs on the water and often by 10 a.m. all the adults are dead and drifting in the back eddies.

LARVA: Trico larva are tiny and pudgy. These little crawlers are generally an olive brown color and have three tails. I don't end up fishing them often because they are most active just before the hatch starts and since that happens early in the morning, I'd have to be nymphing before sunup. If you have a windy morning, the hatch will often get suppressed. Generally speaking, though, the mornings are not the windy part of the day on the Missouri River—but if that does happen, dead-drift a #20 2X short Lovebug, RS-2 or Pheasant Tail under a strike indicator.

DUN: Many of the duns die and never get to reproduce. It's only their sheer numbers that perpetuate the species. These are very fragile creatures, even though they look stout and robust. Sampling the drift will show you that many inexplicably die even before they molt. Fishing very high-riding dry-fly patterns will

sometimes solicit strikes, but a better tactic is to keep the pattern riding very low in the surface film, which means parachute patterns. A Hi-Vis Parachute or a Parachute Adams in a size #22 or #24 works wonders. And for those times when the naturals are clustered together, a #18 or #20 Griffiths Gnat or Buzzball can save the day. Tie on a #14 or #16 PMD Cripple or a #14 Royal Double Wing as an indicator fly and, some days, you will find them ignoring the tiny Trico and keying in on the top fly.

ADULT: I used to tie Clear Winged Spinners for the Trico spinner fall, but I'm not convinced that they work better than the Hi-Vis Parachute. Usually, by the time the spinner fall is on the water in late morning, the fish seem to start keying in on the PMD Cripple or an attractor pattern.

Caddisflies (Trichoptera)

When I was a kid I used to spend a great deal of time with my grandfather. We shared a love of fishing and the outdoors. I remember finding a tube-like object stuck to a rock in a river and asked him what it was. "Periwinkle. There's an insect inside it." I was amazed and peeled the case off to find that indeed there was a live worm-like creature inside. I didn't know at the time that this insect would mature into an adult stage when it would leave its watery world and get airborne.

Grandpa never mentioned this and maybe he didn't know. For a long time, people thought that caddisflies were moths. While they are a close cousin to their land-bound relatives, there are some distinct differences. Caddisflies also are attracted to light and orient themselves to the light source, mistaking it for the moon, and will spend hours orbiting their newfound "moons" trying to regain a sense of balance. These insects also go through what is called a complete metamorphosis of egg, larva, pupa, and adult stages. Unlike moths, however, all but the adult stage occur underwater.

Next to Diptera, Caddis (order Trichoptera) has more different species than any other aquatic insect, with approximately 1,200 in North America. Few generalizations will fit all of them.

Caddisfly adults have four wings, six legs, no tail, and two antennae. When at rest their wings are folded back over their body forming a tent. Shaking the willows or other shore brush will often produce a storm of flying caddis as they like to rest and mate in the protection of trees or brush. Many species will absorb water from the dew or rain on the brush, and some even suck nectar from flowers. And while they are able to live much longer than mayflies, their time as adults is limited, especially for the females who are forced back to the water to lay eggs. Some species drop the eggs on the surface, while others dive to the substrate to deposit eggs. Two of the three main caddis hatches on the Missouri are divers.

Caddis have some interesting behaviors. Some species build a case around their worm-like larva. Then they attach themselves to the substrate and build a web, much like a spider, to capture food forced into it by the current. They can suspend themselves in the current by using a silk-like thread that they attach to a rock or stick. They do this when searching for a new home or better feeding position. Other species are free living, and don't build protective cases until they pupate, but use anal hooks to hold on to the substrate.

After pupation, caddis are better able to float to the surface and escape their water world because there is only a small membrane to break through, while other orders of insects have to break through a rather tough exoskeleton in order to get their

Missouri River trout love dry flies from the tiny midges and Tricos to large terrestrials like this hopper.

wings, legs, and bodies out and fly off. But they still have to dry their bodies and wings, and the trout will often key on them in this very vulnerable emergence stage.

For the fly-fishing angler, one important thing about caddis is that trout mostly take the adult differently than they do a mayfly or midge. Because the caddis is nearly flight-ready when it hits the surface, trout seem to know that they cannot take them as leisurely as a midge or mayfly. If you find yourself wondering what the fish are eating, especially if there is a multiple hatch, and the rises are splashy and aggressive, it's probably the caddis that the trout are keying on.

The Missouri River sees three major caddis hatches: Grannom (*Brachycentrus*), Spotted Sedge (*Hydropsyche*), and "Little Sister" Sedge (*Cheumatopsyche*). Several others occur in smaller numbers and some years can be significant, but the patterns and presentations used for these three will work for the others with the exception of the Giant Orange Sedge (*Dicosmoecus*) that occurs in mid-September through mid-October. Many of the other caddisflies are small and require patterns in sizes #18 and #20.

While winter on the Missouri doesn't always mean snow, ice, and sub-zero temperatures, the hatches are confined to midges.

Grannom
(Brachycentrus)

Two different species of Grannom hatch on the Missouri. The first usually occurs in May and lasts only a few weeks at best. You will often see the adults coming off in mid-afternoon. Some years there are very few, and these insects may not even be seen on the upper river. The second one is in July and generally lasts through August and often occurs early in the morning with the Trico hatch.

LARVA: This case builder has an affinity for rappelling from the substrate using a strand of spider-web-like material. Try marking the last 12" to 18" of your tippet with a white Mean Streak Marker to imitate this behavior, and dead drift a LaFontaine Dark Cased Caddis pattern in a size #14 or #16. Other good patterns are a Natural Hare's Ear or Brassie.

PUPA: The case is closed off during this

stage and when finished, the insect has wings, antennae, and legs drawn back over its body encased in a semi-transparent membrane filled with air. Pupa can be free in the drift for some time before they emerge. Fishing pupa patterns dead-drifted along the bottom is often the most productive way to catch trout actively feeding on caddis. Often you can nymph fish in this manner for a few hours before you ever see an adult emerge. The best patterns are a Brown and Bright Green LaFontaine Deep Sparkle Pupa in sizes #14 and #16, a Peacock Soft Hackle, or a Sparkle Caddis.

EMERGER: After cutting its way out of the pupal case, the Grannom floats upward, but it often takes many minutes before it breaks through the surface film, ruptures the sheath at the thorax, climbs out, dries its wings, and flies off. The sheath emits air bubbles which, combined with the struggling motion, solicit fierce strikes by the fish. Use a Brown and Bright Green LaFontaine Sparkle Emerger in a size #16.

ADULT: After emerging, the adults may ride the surface for a time drying their wings. This stage is best imitated with a Henryville or Elk Hair Caddis in size #14 or #16 with dark green body and brown wings.

EGG LAYING AND SPENT: The females deposit their eggs on the substrate and consequently find themselves frantically swim-

> Generally speaking, if you see dorsals and tails, the fish are eating just below the surface. Fish don't have brakes. If they are chasing a caddis as it's floating to the surface, their momentum often will carry them out of the water after they've captured their prey. Look closely to see if their mouths are open or closed. If closed, they are probably not eating something on the surface. Look for that open mouth. If you see the crown of the head or nose breach the surface with an open mouth, they are feeding on the adult dries. A good pair of binoculars will let you see this behavior close up. Once you observe the difference a few times, you will learn what to look for.

ming to achieve their final mission. Besides a few soft hackle patterns, the only pattern I know of to imitate this behavior is a LaFontaine Diving Caddis. Use it in brown and green in a size #14 or #16 and fish it very actively. The spent caddis imitates the dead insect. The wings of the natural are often in a delta formation, but sometimes are not symmetrical. A Lawson Spent Partridge Caddis is effective as well as a Delta Wing Caddis in sizes #14 and #16.

Spotted Sedge
(Hydropsyche)

This caddis lives freely in the water without a case for protection except when it pupates. If you find the larva, they will look much like worms with legs under the thorax. The adults have a distinctly spotted wing. In the heat of the summer, they emerge when daily temperatures are cooler. Normally, you'll start seeing this caddis in mid-July and it will continue until early October.

LARVA: These insects won't show up in a seine very often and you might get the impression that not very many are present. Their ability to anchor themselves to a rock or stick by using a silk-like anchor line ensures that they stay secured to the bottom. They gather food by building small nets that collect both animal and plant material. The fish will sometimes pick them off if they find them trying to move from one feeding site to another.

Spotted sedges do get dislodged, though, and using the Mean Streak Marker often will trigger strikes if the nymph alone does not work. Caddis are not good swimmers, except in the adult stage, so dead-drift all imitations. Use a LaFontaine Olive/Brown Caddis Larva pattern in a size #14 or #16. Other good patterns are a Natural or Olive Hare's Ear.

PUPA: A cocoon is built for pupation, then afterwards, they will often drift freely inside the sheath as gasses build that will carry them upward. They often hang just underneath the surface film for long periods of time before finally breaking free of the sheath. I've watched them in slow moving water and it's like they are stuck inside a balloon that they can't break because each time they kick the sheath gives. Gary LaFontaine used to tell of caddis emergers he timed at over an hour before they finally broke free and flew away. They are very vulnerable at this stage and the trout can't seem to resist that struggle. The best patterns are a Brown and Olive LaFontaine Deep Sparkle Pupa in size #14 and #16 and a Peacock Soft Hackle.

EMERGER: Dead-drift a Brown and Tan LaFontaine Sparkle Emerger in a size #16 with an occasional twitch.

ADULT: Deer hair best imitates the natural wing color but it is harder to see than bleached elk hair. My favorites are a Deer Hair Caddis, Henryville, and Lawson's Spent Wing in a size #14 or #16 with a dirty yellow or tan body.

EGG LAYING OR SPENT: After the females lay their eggs they often float to the surface, but die without ever flying off. A LaFontaine Brown and Tan Diving caddis in a #14 or #16 for the egg layers, and a Lawson Spent Partridge Caddis as well as a Delta Wing Caddis in sizes #14 and #16 for the dead females on the surface.

Choosing the right pattern means understanding something about the hatches and is all part of the challenge and joy of the sport.

Little Sister Sedge
(Cheumatopsyche)

It's called the Little Sister Sedge because it's a close relative to the *Hydropsyche*. Many years ago it was included in the same genus. I have seen this hatch on other rivers, where it occurs much earlier in the year and the insects are darker, probably so they can absorb sunlight better in the colder waters. On the Missouri, this hatch generally starts in June and lasts until around Labor Day. It's important because it tends to be the predominant evening hatch in the warmer months.

LARVA: This free-living caddis is normally about one size smaller than the Grannom and the Spotted Sedge. The larva find a feeding place on the bottom and make a small web-like net to catch food that is free in the drift. Imitate the larva with a LaFontaine Olive Tan Caddis Larva in size #16 and #18 or a Tan Hare's Ear.

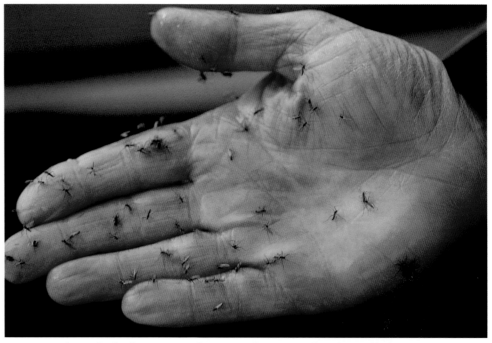

When midge hatches occur in early spring on the Missouri, they often are blanket hatches with clusters of insects. Cluster imitations work well in this situation.

PUPA: Like its cousin, the spotted sedge, the little sister builds a cocoon around itself to pupate. When finished, it cuts its way out of the cocoon and rides the currents, often for a few hours, before emerging by riding the gas-filled sheath to the surface. You have to get this nymph dead-drifted on or very near the bottom to catch fish. Use a LaFontaine Brown and Tan Deep Sparkle Pupa in sizes #16 and #18. A Tan Hare's Ear Soft Hackle can also be very effective in the same sizes. When you start to see trout actively feeding on the insects just below the surface, you may find yourself getting most of your strikes on the swing.

EMERGER: They are clumsy and vulnerable when they hit the bottom of the surface film, often riding it for long periods of time—some estimates say hours—before they break through and fly off. This is often a very confusing time for fly fishermen.

They see that the fish are active on the surface but won't take an adult dry fly. It took me many days on the water to realize that the only strikes came when my dry fly was drowned. The answer is to show most of your pattern below the surface. Use a LaFontaine Brown and Tan Sparkle Emerger in a size #16 or #18, and put floatant only on the top of the wing. This allows the fly to sit lower, which better imitates the struggling insect.

ADULT: The females return to the water after mating to oviposit (lay eggs). I have not observed this behavior very often, and suspect it may occur after dark. A Lawson Spent Wing Caddis or a Delta Wing Caddis in sizes #16 and #18 with ginger body and tan wings works well, but I'm not convinced the trout are taking it for the adult egg layers or for stillborn adults that never made it out of the protective sheath. Since this activity often happens when it's nearly dark it's difficult to observe. But as my brother once said, "Who the hell cares? They're eating it aren't they?" Good point.

Giant Orange Sedge, October Caddis
(Dicosmoecus)

This is not a major hatch on the Missouri, and it's one of those where you have to be at the right place at the right time. But when it happens to you, it's worth the wait. These are the largest of the caddis and they hatch in the fall when the large predatory browns are beginning to get the spawning itch. From mid-September to mid-October, after the sun is off the water, you will sometimes hear big splashy rises and occasionally see these "B-52s" against the glow of the setting sun. It's a time to catch very large trout, especially large browns on a dry fly.

LARVA: This sedge larva is so large that you might not believe there is really an insect inside. You'll often find them clinging to rocks early in the season in slow-moving water. As water temperatures heat up, they set out for faster and cooler water, often shedding their cases to swim and feed freely in the current. While I know that trout eat them encased, I've had better luck fishing a LaFontaine Yellow Caddis Larva in a size #8.

PUPA: During pupation, this genus goes into a somewhat dormant period that can last for weeks. Until the pupae emerge from their cases they are not often available to the fish. I've only seen the pupa moving to the surface once and it looked like an obese dog frantically trying to waddle its way along. Its legs were pumping like mad but they didn't move very fast, possibly due to its large size. There isn't as much information about these giant caddis as there is on the other species but I have read about steelhead—and even Pacific salmon—rising to these bad boys, so it's obvious that they catch the attention of very large fish. Use a Brown and Orange Deep Sparkle Pupa in a size #8 or #10.

EMERGER: A Brown and Orange Sparkle Emerger with a deer hair wing in a size #8 is the best pattern I have found.

ADULT: This is the fun part. When the emergers/adults struggle to dry their wings after freeing themselves from the sheaths, they are very clumsy and slow. Like a goose, they often seem to be running on the water surface for some time before they get airborne. I've taken dry patterns and swung them across weed beds and had four or five strikes with chasing and slashing trout going after the pattern. It will make you giddy watching this behavior. But normally, a dead-drift is your best method. Use a burnt orange variation of a Bucktail Caddis in a size #8 or #10.

True Flies (Diptera)

Midges belong to the family Chironomidae, which is part of the order known to entomologists as Diptera. This order is huge, with thousands of species with varying characteristics. Mosquitoes are part of this order, as are craneflies. Many midges look and act much like a mosquito but don't need your blood to feed their young. A mosquito is sort of like a midge with an attitude.

Midges—normally small, two-winged aquatic insects—are sometimes called snowflies because they can often be seen actively hatching, flying, and mating in the winter. Their life cycle begins with eggs on the bottom of the river. Next is the larval stage, when they look much like very thin housefly maggots, their non-aquatic cousins. Because they are very small, many anglers question midges' worth, but trout, particularly wintering trout, eat them with abandon. It's one of the few food sources available to them during the cold months.

After the larval stage, midges mostly pupate within the somewhat hardened capsule of the larva. After a relatively short pupation, they rise to the surface. Emergence is often slow in the winter months, and it may take minutes for them to dry and harden their new wings for flight. This is usually done while they are standing on the discarded pupal shuck. Often, large groups of

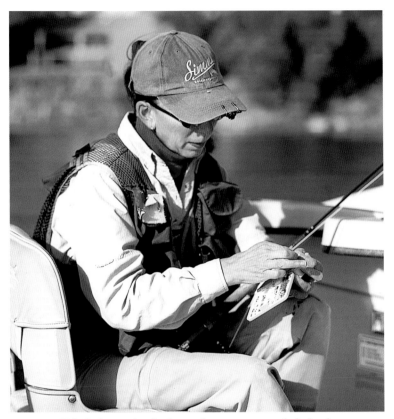

Nola Krahe searches for that perfect pattern to match the hatch.

midges cling to each other as they struggle in their pre-flight tasks. These clusters of squiggling insects are frequently what trigger trout to feed on the surface. Finding such clusters also offers the prepared angler a tremendous advantage. A single winter midge on the Missouri is probably a size #20 to #26; a cluster of these little guys can be imitated with a size #14.

A magnificent cluster imitation is Gary LaFontaine's Buzzball. It is tied in a size #14 or #16, and it magically drops the IQ of feeding fish. Initially, its only drawback was that it was hard to see, so Gary, being a very innovative genius, added a white Antron® wing. Many January days have found me stand-

ing knee-deep in the Missouri, catching fish after fish on this pattern. I would pause for a moment, turn toward Deer Lodge, Montana, and pay homage to the wacky king of offbeat patterns. While Gary is best known for his work with caddisflies, he must have had an epiphany when he came up with the Buzzball. If you find yourself on the river this time of year without this pattern, a Griffith's Gnat will also work—but not nearly as well. The feeding frenzy often won't last more than an hour, but it will be the hour you talk about for a long time. Catching big Missouri River browns and 'bows on dry flies in mid-winter in Montana isn't an ordinary event, so it will be burned into your memory long after you've forgotten countless computer passwords.

When fishing subsurface patterns, you'll have to keep them small. One way to keep the hook size bigger than what would normally fit the pattern is to tie it on a short-shank hook. By using a 2X short hook you can make the pattern appear one size smaller while retaining the hooking power of the larger hook. A client once asked me if the trout might not be put off from this larger hook. I replied that if it weren't for the fact that a trout ignores the piece of metal sticking out the butt of its supposed food, no one would ever be able to catch a fish on a fly.

Two very good patterns for midges while nymphing are the Lovebug and the Serendipity. Other nymph patterns that can be highly effective are the Zebra Nymph, Lightning Bug, RS-2 ,and WD-40s in sizes #20 to #26. All of these patterns can also work well as a dropper off a dry fly to imitate the emerging midge.

Midges might be the most challenging of fly patterns. Because of the insects' small size, trout are rarely fooled by patterns that are too large or too bulky. Stick with the simple patterns that show the fish a slender profile. While midges come in many different colors, best on the Missouri are shades of gray, olive, and red.

LARVA: Most genera of this family are very small. If you screen them from the river they may be mistaken for something else.

Close inspection will reveal a slight segmentation to the worm-like body. Their lack of tails and their small antennae make them easy to distinguish from Mayfly larva. By keeping your patterns small and sparsely dubbed, you'll better imitate the natural. A #18 to #22 Serendipity tied on a 2X short hook in red, olive, or gray is one of the best patterns, especially in winter. There are hundreds of midge patterns and many of them will work well if you keep them thin and simple.

PUPA: I tend to mimic this stage most often. The naturals are more active just after they pupate, which will happen most days during the year somewhere on the river. The midges are more active during this stage and present better feeding opportunities to the trout. The pupae look much like the larva except that they are a little bigger and have distinct wing pads that are clumped together with the thorax and head. Often you will have gill fibers extending above and forward of the thorax. The Serendipity works even better for this stage in the same size and colors as used for the Larva. A Lovebug, RS-2 (olive or gray), WD-40 (olive or brown), black Zebra Nymph, and Lightning Bug will work if you keep them sparse and smaller than a #18 and tied on Scud hooks.

ADULTS: As the midges reach maturity, it seems that the body colors in colder months are mostly dark, probably to better absorb sunlight. While they still lack tails, their wings have emerged and are folded over their bodies when at rest. The antennae are small. Imitations can be made to mimic a single midge and those patterns are a #20 to #26 Hi-Vis Parachute in gray and olive or even an Adams in the same sizes. My preference is to imitate the clusters as these squirming balls seem to attract more trout and make hooking them much easier. Use a #14 to #16 La Fontaine Hi-vis Buzzball or a #16 to #20 Griffiths Gnat.

Stoneflies (Plecoptera)

Tailwaters are not good habitat for most stoneflies and the Missouri isn't the exception. You will find, from time to time, some hatches of green stoneflies (*Sweltsa*) that can be matched with some of the Yellow Sally patterns or Yellow Stimulators, but these hatches are haphazard most years. There are also some golden stones (*Calineuria*, formerly *Acroneuria*) on the lower river, but there aren't the sheer numbers that the midges, caddis, and mayflies offer. And while I've seen salmonflies and skwalas, they are few and may have originated in the Dearborn River and were washed down.

Terrestrials

Grasshoppers

It was a picture perfect early fall day. The temperatures were in the 70s and it was sunny. I had gotten my driver's license only a few months before and my dad loaned me his car. I was new to dating and girls were a complete mystery to me since I went to an all-boys high school. I knew they smelled better, and I was anxious to learn more. Much more. My girlfriend was Linda and she lived in a small town called Penrose. I picked her up and we went for a picnic near the Arkansas River. I thought if the date went badly I could still catch a few fish, plus the trunk of my dad's Impala was full of gear. She was a beautiful girl who later became a beauty queen and just seeing her quickened my pulse, just not quite as much as hooking some big brown on a Renegade.

We arrived at the river about lunchtime and she had this huge picnic basket with fried chicken and Nehi grape pop. I threw down an old woolen Army blanket on the grass and we had a good time sitting in the fall sun eating and talking about who knows what.

A grasshopper landed on the blanket, and I reached out to swat it away and realized it was stuck to the blanket. I picked it up but it took a bit of untangling to get its barbed back legs free of the wool. Fascinated by this quirk of science, I threw him back on the blanket and he stuck again. My biology teacher, Father Hallenbach, told me that an experiment had to be repeatable by another scientist, but I couldn't get Linda to throw the grasshopper that was now drooling some green stuff. I took the blanket and started dragging it through the grass, snaring more hoppers along with cactus and burrs.

I collected the hoppers from the blanket and stuffed them into a bait can. Linda and I sat on a rock and I pitched them into the river. Within minutes the trout were lining up to join the feast. I took out my rod and impaled a few on bait hooks and had fun catching them, but the real value of this discovery was just how crazy trout got over hoppers.

Later, Griz and I perfected the collection method by putting the blanket over the front of the car and driving through hay fields. We then stored them in one of those gallon pickle jars.

Lots of grasses grow along the banks of the Missouri, and hoppers seem to reproduce well in this environment. They often find themselves being blown off course and into the water where the fish, particularly on the lower river, wait for them.

Insects can break through the surface film easier in broken water and fish normally will be a bit less selective.

I have fished all sorts of patterns from foam-bodied to the most intricate, but the one pattern that fills the bill year in and year out is a variant of a Parachute Hopper. Foam bodies made the fly look artificial and dubbed bodies made it sink. Dave Whitlock's patterns worked pretty well but they took a long time to tie. As a guide I needed something I could tie quickly at 4 am. My pattern uses an underbody of foam and an overbody of dubbing. I added Krystal flash as an underwing.

Trout will often bump a hopper to see if it wiggles. Using a Rapala knot will allow the fly to move when bumped if you don't tie the dropper off the bend of the hook. This rigging is detailed later in this chapter.

This pattern's productivity is probably due to the fact that the most productive hopper days are when it's at least a little windy. The wind ruffles the water surface, and high-riding patterns don't get noticed as well as the parachute style that sits low in the surface film. At times, the takes are very subtle and, if you are gazing around at the scenery, you may turn to notice that you can't locate your fly—which a bank feeding trout has ambushed. Other times a violent explosion surrounding your fly will surprise you.

Hopper fishing on the Missouri is exciting. Fish them close to the banks, dead-drifted and under overhanging foliage and grasses during the hot summer months of July, August, and sometimes early September. Another good place to present your hopper imitation is over fairly shallow weed beds. Trout will sit in the small slits of weed beds and bushwhack the hoppers as they struggle overhead. Often times you can see the fish flash deep and near the bottom and then watch as it ascends to the fly. The hard part is not setting the hook prematurely. Usually after the first hard frost or snow, the hopper fishing is over for the year. Some years there just aren't many naturals on the banks and the trout are mostly uninterested in them. Often during the summer a hopper will also make a great strike indicator for a nymph dropper. Even dropper flies as large as a San Juan Worm can be used.

Beetles

The natural hoppers don't show up until the weather is warm, but beetles are around from April through October most years. They don't solicit the hard strikes like hoppers, but they often get fish to eat when nothing else works. Fish a #14 or #16 Black Foam Beetle with a Hi-Vis wing to make it easier for you to see, or drop the fly off a #12 Royal Double wing or a #10 Parachute Hopper Variant.

Streamers

There are all sorts of small baitfish on the Missouri from whitefish fingerlings to sculpins. Many crayfish also make a home on this tailwater. If you decide to wet wade in the heat of the summer, especially in grassy slow-moving water, you might discover the abundant leeches that look at your bare legs as an invitation to dinner. They are easily picked off and, while I've seen leeches in the two-inch range, I've rarely picked any off my legs that were larger than half an inch. I think at times the fish might take our small Zebra nymphs for this naturally occurring food. Specific pattern imitations can be very effective, but most of the seasoned veterans carry a large supply of Wooly Buggers. It seems that everyone has their own variations including beadheads, Krystal Flash, rubber legs, and weighted, but the colors mostly come down to olive, brown, and black. With those three colors in sizes #2 to #10 you will ordinarily entice large predatory trout to your fly. Keep in mind that not every day is a good Bugger day. For reasons unknown, trout will often ignore a large fly and key in on #22 Tricos.

Presenting a streamer in the classic "quarter downstream" method will entice fish but often a dead-drift works just as well, if not better. Trout will often ram the fly with the crowns of their heads first. This is done to stun the baitfish so that it may be eaten headfirst and the fins do not choke the predator going down his gullet.

If you feel the strike and raise the rod tip, the fly is too far away from the fish for him to take it a second time. In his world, it just disappears. A much better method is to use a strip set. When you feel the strike, pull the line very hard, an arm's length. Then, if you don't hook the fish, it's still within his range. And when you stop pulling and reach up for the line again, the fly will flutter and begin to sink, the same thing a natural baitfish would do if stunned. Keep stripping the line in slowly and use more strip sets until the fish is hooked. I once had a fish hit it twelve times before I finally hooked him on the thirteenth strip set.

When the light conditions are right, you can sight-fish those bank huggers in shallow water. Putting the streamer in front of the target will often get his attention. You'll know when you see this "Cruise missile" turn to follow the target in acquisition mode. Some ethereal GPS coordinates are fed into its tiny brain and it makes course corrections as it accelerates to the target. The final explosion happens when nose hits target. The picture will stay emblazoned in your memory for subsequent water cooler discussions.

Nymphing

Technique

The best technique for successful nymphing in any tailwater, but the Missouri in particular, is to first understand the habitat. Water velocity below dams is slowed. Runoff will only shut down the fishery in those extreme years where the dams are full and water flows heavily over the spillways and through the waste gates. It's then that extreme high water is seen, and even that doesn't have the scouring effect that occurs each spring on freestone rivers.

Tailwaters often have pampered substrates where aquatic grasses and weeds are free to grow unhindered by fierce spring runoffs that tend to purge vegetation once a year. The Missouri is such a tailwater, and that's why many see it as a spring creek on steroids. These grasses further moderate the water's velocity.

Illustration by Mark Lewis

The structure on the bottom of the river causes a turbulence in the water. Getting your flies to the bottom and keeping them drag free will ensure more hookups. When the trout's head is down he's looking for nymphs. When it's up he is looking at the surface.

This Blue Ribbon section of the Missouri has very little visible, above the surface, structure and so the normal runs and pools are harder to detect. If what you mostly fish are freestone rivers with lots of rocks and logs, it makes reading this river look like cracking computer program code. Fortunately, with a little information and some practice, this code is easier to understand. The structure is there, it just looks different—it looks like aquatic grasses. These grasses break the speed of the current, provide protection from predators, and are casino buffets of trout food. For the most part, in this section of the river, when you get away from the weed beds, you get away from the trout and into the whitefish.

Drag

The key to successfully fishing this water is to be drag free. Everything that is free in the drift moves at a very predictable speed and the fish have spent a lifetime becoming accustomed to that speed. Dragging your flies, even micro drag, will stand out like Madonna at an Amish barn-raising.

Drag is when your flies, nymphs or dries, move at a speed that doesn't match that of the natural insects or current. It doesn't matter if the flies are going faster or slower than the current, it's still drag and drag is bad. On a freestone river, there is normally lots of structure, and the currents and eddies are pulling the natural food different directions. So, a quick shift in direction isn't all that alarming for the fish. On the Missouri, most of the current moves along at a predictable pace, and drag can't be forgiven. If you're dragging your flies you're just working out your casting arm and mostly catching whitefish.

When nymphing, eliminating drag starts with your equipment. The most neglected piece of equipment is usually the fly line. A generation or two ago, men took meticulous care with their fly lines because they were very expensive. Made of silk,

Catch and Release

- Smash your barbs. This alone will cut your hooking mortality in half.
- Don't play a fish to exhaustion.
- Use a quick release device to release the fish without lifting it from the water.
- Use a rubber or other knotless net.
- Don't take the fish out of the water.
- If you must touch the fish, do it with wet hands but don't push it against waders or vest.
- To revive an exhausted fish, face it upstream in current, until it swims from your hand.
- If there is little current, swim the fish around in circles rather than a back and forth motion.
- Don't hold the fish over anything but water to prevent dropping injury.
- Cover the trout's eyes with your wet hand to calm it when removing a hook.

they required daily maintenance. Today, fly line is mostly some sort of hollow tube of polymer–plastic. And most of us see plastic as something very durable, long lasting and low maintenance. Small particles of decomposed vegetation and stream detritus cling to the fly line. After it dries it becomes an added layer and the next time the line is used it accumulates more dirt. This adds weight to the line and friction against the guides. A clean fly line floats well but also moves through the rod guides with much less effort, and this is the key to good mending techniques (see below). If the line hangs in the guides, mending technique goes down the toilet. Instead of fighting the dirty fly line for nine or ten hours each day, a five-minute cleaning is a good investment.

The cure for drag while nymphing is called "mending." Mending is when you lift the fly line up and throw it upstream of the indicator. This helps to eliminate drag because the velocity of the water on the surface is greater than the velocity of the water on or near the bottom. The reason is because the substrate (bottom of the river) has rocks, grasses, etc., that offer resistance to the current. The fly line that you have out on the water is forming a downstream belly and, as the line tightens, the indicator accelerates and moves downstream faster than your flies. When this happens your flies are dragging, and an upstream mend is needed. Then as the indicator and flies continue to drift downstream, you can feed some slack line to extend how long your flies are near the bottom. When the fly line tightens, the flies will lift off the bottom and it's time to cast again.

Rigging

First, tie in a two-foot-long, 40-pound butt section to your fly line with a nail or needle knot. Using a blood knot, tie a 9-foot 3X knotless leader to the butt section. Now, using another blood knot, add 3 feet of 3X tippet to the leader. Here are three different ways to tie on the two-nymph setup *(see graphic this page)*.

A fly with a 3/32" tungsten bead is ideal for the top fly. A #10 red San Juan Worm or a #14 Pink Scud is a great all-around choice. If you tie a spark plug on your tippet to get the flies to the bottom, it will hang and slow the flies. Enough weight to get the flies down and not so much as to hang the bottom all the time is the solution. Tungsten beads are a great solution when using a two-fly rig in moderate moving water, but keep a supply of split shot for heavier current.

Strike indicators are very useful, particularly when fishing uniformly moving currents with small nymphs. When a trout takes a small fly, he's not going to call his mom and tell her what a prize he just found. Instead he's going to either eat it or expel it with little fanfare and will not often move after taking it. This action by the trout will often only cause the indicator to stutter for a moment. Without a strike indicator, many subtle strikes will be missed.

#1

#2

#3

1. Tie an improved Clinch knot to the top fly, tie an 18" to 24" section of tippet with a second improved Clinch to the bend of the hook, and a third to the dropper fly on the other end of the tippet.
2. Tie an improved Clinch knot to the top fly but leave the tag end untrimmed. Then, with a blood knot, tie an 18" to 24" second section of 4X tippet to the untrimmed tag end. Use an improved Clinch to tie on the dropper fly.
3. Tie a Rapalla knot to the top fly, and the dropper on as in #1 or #2.

Illustrations by Mark Lewis

Position your strike indicator at two times the water depth. Besides drag, positioning the indicator at merely the water depth is the most common mistake fly fishers make. The flies do not hang perpendicular to your indicator, but rather the current and different water velocities at the surface and the bottom cause the line to arc. The water velocity at the bottom is less because structure slows the current, tumbling the water and anything drifting along the bottom. This tends to lift the flies off the bottom, and then they drift over the heads of the fish you are tying to catch.

Because you are using a minimum amount of weight to get the flies down to the sweet spot, thus better mimicking the naturals, it takes longer to get them from the surface to the bottom. An up-stream cast is necessary, followed by a good mend (see above). If you are fishing a tight line, you are likely dragging your flies.

Presentation

While wade fishing, the best approach is to cast about 45° upstream in most currents. When casting in a faster moving current, go higher—and in slower currents, move more towards straight across. Your flies will sink much more slowly than you imagine. If you want an eye opener, find a swimming pool and throw a penny in and then count the seconds until it hits the bottom. When you cast into water that is moving, if you don't cast the fly upstream you won't get a long enough drift to get the flies down to the bottom, and that is where trout eat nymphs. After casting, allow the flies to sink and when the indicator is across from you, mend.

Be aware that when the flies lift and begin to swing toward the surface, they can often imitate the natural insects as they emerge, and fish will often strike these flies just before the hatch. When they do this, it's called "a take on the swing." This also serves as a signal that the hatch may be about to become visible.

Strategies

Like people standing in an elevator, trout will solemnly face the same direction—up-current. Up-current is different than upstream because islands and other structure at times will alter the current's direction. A back eddy is a good example. The fish in a back eddy may be facing downstream on one part, and upstream in another part. The current acts like a huge conveyor belt that delivers the squirming larva and pupae. While some aquatic insects can swim, few can manage against even the slightest of currents. It's worth noting which direction the fish are facing, because the best hook sets are perpendicular to that direction. If a fish is facing upstream and you set the hook upstream, you will likely pull the fly from his mouth or get a bad hook set. This is because we can never know how the fly will be oriented in the fish's mouth. If the fly is oriented lengthwise along the hook in the fish's mouth, an upstream set will often work. If the orientation is anything other than that, the fly will often be pulled out of the fish's mouth without ever connecting. This is especially true with a small pattern. When the hook is set perpendicular to the fish, the hook has double the opportunities to connect because now it can connect to the top or bottom of the mouth, but also to the side.

It doesn't take trout long to realize that your fly is a fraud. They are like toddlers as they determine the edible things of the world first by sight and/or curiosity, but then by taste. During the normal course of their day they take in and spit out more than they consume. And, like a toddler with a spoonful of mashed broc-

> ## Tip
> Many reels will spin freely in the take-up direction and you can put excess slack on the reel faster by spinning the palming rim with your hand like a top. It's faster than turning the reel with the handle, but don't forget to make the fish your focus.

coli, it doesn't take them long to expel it. To get good hook sets you have to be faster than a mongoose with a belly full of lattés and you have to set in the right direction. Upstream hook sets will pull the fly from the fish as he's trying to spit it out. You have to be fast because it takes time for the take to be telegraphed up to the indicator and, by the time the indicator moves, the fish is often in the process of spitting out the hook. This method is for nymphing. For dry flies or streamers, the hook sets are somewhat different.

In order to get good drag-free drifts that will present the fly properly to the fish, you have to have enough slack in your line. In order to get good hook sets you have to get pressure on to the hook. So, before you can set the hook, you first have to deal with all that slack you just laid out on the water. Keeping your "finger on the trigger" accomplishes this. This means that you put the fly line between your index finger and the cork of the rod. When you feed line out, release the pressure. When you set the hook, press the line firmly to the cork and lift your rod up and perpendicular to the current to set the hook.

Playing the Fish

Rod tips are what protect the light tippet from breaking and light wire hooks from straightening. When the fish pulls, the rod tip gives. It's up to you to let the rod do what it is designed to do. This is accomplished by keeping the rod tip high and allowing slack to slide through your trigger finger when the fish pulls, or stripping slack line in if the fish charges toward you. Too much tension and the fish will break off, too little and they will throw the fly. The biggest mistake is to employ the Vulcan Death Grip. This is when you drive the fly line about a half an inch into the cork of your rod and refuse to give any slack when the fish is heading away from you like a Sidewinder missile. A variation is when you point the rod at the fish and then employ the Vulcan Death Grip. It won't have a happy ending because you've not only lost your flies, but you've also tagged the fish with some pierced body art that he will have to dislodge.

Do this exercise: after your rod is strung, have someone hold

Nymph Patterns

Lovebug

Hook: Scud hook TMC 2457, sizes #18 to #22
Bead: 2mm on sizes #18 and #20
Thread: 8/0 iron gray or dark gray
Tail: A single strand of tinsel, shank length
Underbody: Iron gray thread
Body: Stripped grizzle hackle stem
Rib: Fine gold wire
Thorax: Natural beaver
Emergent wing: Hungarian partridge
Note: This versatile pattern works well as a midge nymph imitation all year long but is particularly effective in the winter months. It also is a great small mayfly imitation the other three seasons.
Originator: Trapper Badovinac

Pink Scud

Hook: Scud hook TMC 2457, sizes #12 to #18
Bead: 3/32" tungsten for the #12 and #14 sizes
Thread: 8/0 pink
Tail: Pink marabou
Body: Orvis pink scud dubbing or equivalent
Shellback: Plastic bag cut into strips
Rib: Gold wire
Note: This pattern works well for the dying scuds, but may best imitate the fish roe. The shellback is optional but seems to work better without.
Originator: Unknown

your rod with the Vulcan Death Grip as you pull on the line. Have them raise the rod tip high and after a few pulls to get the feel of it, have them point the rod tip at you. It's an eye opener. After you hook up a fish, especially if there is heavy current, fly fishing gets paradoxical. The harder you hang on, the less you

Nymph Patterns

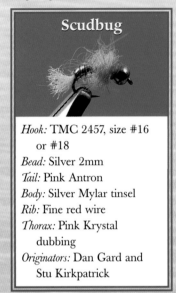

Scudbug

Hook: TMC 2457, size #16 or #18
Bead: Silver 2mm
Tail: Pink Antron
Body: Silver Mylar tinsel
Rib: Fine red wire
Thorax: Pink Krystal dubbing
Originators: Dan Gard and Stu Kirkpatrick

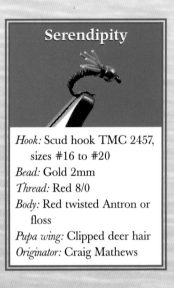

Serendipity

Hook: Scud hook TMC 2457, sizes #16 to #20
Bead: Gold 2mm
Thread: Red 8/0
Body: Red twisted Antron or floss
Pupa wing: Clipped deer hair
Originator: Craig Mathews

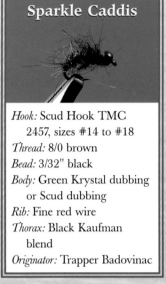

Sparkle Caddis

Hook: Scud Hook TMC 2457, sizes #14 to #18
Thread: 8/0 brown
Bead: 3/32" black
Body: Green Krystal dubbing or Scud dubbing
Rib: Fine red wire
Thorax: Black Kaufman blend
Originator: Trapper Badovinac

Woody

Hook: Scud Hook TMC 2457, size #16 or #18
Bead: 2mm gold
Thread: 8/0 brown
Tail: Lemon Wood Duck
Body: Thread
Shellback: Lemon Wood Duck
Rib: Gold wire
Thorax: Light brown Haretron dubbing
Wingcase: Lemon Wood Duck
Legs: Lemon Wood Duck
Originator: Trapper Badovinac

have. A two-pound trout planing sideways in heavy current weighs as much as a Chevy big-block engine. If you muscle the fish, you will lose. The first thing to do is guide the fish out of the current. This is accomplished by moving the rod tip so that the fly line is perpendicular to the current. This turns the fish's head and the current will push, or plane, the fish toward you. Some fish may require your patience for a moment or two before they swing toward you and out of the current. The amount of pressure to give the fish will depend on the size of the fish, the strength of the current, the size of your fly, tippet size, and other factors. When applying pressure think of it as "encouragement" to the fish to leave the current rather than "insistence."

Playing the fish off the reel means that you've either wound the slack line back onto the reel or the fish has pulled the slack out as it ran away from you, or some of both. This is when a good drag is important. If your drag is set correctly, you can now release your finger from the trigger and let the reel do the work. When the fish pulls, the reel will allow line to come off the spool and, when the fish comes toward you, the slack line is then stripped if the fish is coming fast, or wound on the reel while you keep your rod tip in the proper position. There are ways to "play the line" with one hand when the fish is on the reel, but it requires some demonstration and practice. The same is true for "palming" the reel. You can control the tension on the fish by creating friction with your fingers to add to the drag of the reel.

The actions a fly fisher takes after the fish is hooked will determine whether the fish will likely die or live. The Catch and Release chapter of this book has detailed information about how to minimize your impact on the resource, but a few quick tips are shown in the "Catch and Release" sidebar on page 82.

Nymph Patterns

Hit & Run

Hook: Scud hook TMC 2457, sizes #16 to #20
Bead: Gold 2mm
Thread: Brown 8/0
Tail: Hungarian partridge
Body: Red halographic tinsel
Rib: 3X tippet wound brassie style
Thorax: Light brown hare's ear dubbing
Wing case: Hungarian partridge
Legs: Hungarian partridge
Originator: Trapper Badovinac

Lightening Bug

Hook: Scud hook TMC 2457, sizes #16 to #20
Bead: Gold 2mm
Thread: Olive
Tail: Pheasant tail
Body: Gold or silver halographic tinsel
Rib: Wire to match
Thorax: Peacock herl
Originator: Unknown

San Juan Worm

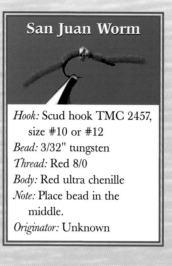

Hook: Scud hook TMC 2457, size #10 or #12
Bead: 3/32" tungsten
Thread: Red 8/0
Body: Red ultra chenille
Note: Place bead in the middle.
Originator: Unknown

RS-2

Hook: Scud hook TMC 2457, sizes #18 to #22
Bead: 2mm on sizes #18 and #20
Tail: Olive microfibbets
Body: Olive beaver
Wing: Dark brown or black hackle webbing
Note: This also works in tan and gray.
Originator: Rim Chung

Dry Flies

Technique

From Holter Dam to Cascade, the Missouri River is an easy-going trout stream most years. You won't find any spectacular water falls or deep gorges. Consequently, the fish are used to seeing their food delivered at a fairly slow pace, and having time to scrutinize whatever comes into view. For successful dry fly fishing days on this river, you can't be sloppy.

When approaching rising fish, move slowly. If possible, keep your profile down and against a river bank instead of the sky. Wear clothing that blends with the colors of the foliage and remove any shiny jewelry or watches.

Large trout will feed on the river's heavy hatches with abandon if they feel they are not being threatened. Trico, Midge, and Pseudo hatches bring trout to the surface, where they hold while they feed on these small insects. But the fish remain super spooky at this time. If you approach them with large splashy movements, or if you false cast over the top of them, they will spook. You will be better off to take the extra time to get within casting distance, rather than spook them and then spend the next 20 minutes waiting for them to come back up.

Drag

Drag is bad while nymphing and it's *really* bad when fishing dry flies. And if it's really bad when fishing dry flies on a free-stone river, it's virtually suicidal on a tailwater fishery like the Missouri. If the fish see even the slightest of wakes, they will refuse your fly. If your fly is leaving a wake that a jet skier would be proud of, you are wasting your time.

Dry Fly Patterns

Parachute Hopper Variant

Hook: 2xl, 1xf TMC 5212, size #10
Thread: Tan 8/0
Underbody: Yellow foam, segmented with thread
Overbody: Tan Haretron dubbing
Legs: Pheasant tail
Underwing: Krystal Flash
Wing: Turkey quill
Post: White Antron
Thorax: Tan Haretron
Hackle: Grizzly
Originator: Trapper Badovinac

PMD Emerger

Hook: Standard Dry TMC 101, sizes #16 & #18
Thread: 8/0 brown
Tail: Pheasant tail
Body: Wrapped pheasant tail
Rib: Gold wire
Thorax: Pheasant tail
Dubbing ball: White Antron
Hackle: Medium dun, parachute style
Originator: Unknown

PMD Cripple

Hook: Standard Dry TMC 100 or 101, sizes #14 to #18
Thread: 8/0 brown
Tail: Pheasant tail
Body: Pheasant tail
Rib: Gold wire
Thorax: Yellow Haretron dubbing
Wing: Coastal deer hair
Hackle: Barred light ginger
Originator: Quigley

LaFontaine Royal Double Wing

Hook: Standard Dry TMC 100 or 101, size #14 or #16
Thread: 8/0 brown
Tip: Red floss
Tail: Combed out light olive Antron
Rear wing: Bear, brown
Body: Peacock herl
Body hackle: Brown rooster, clipped top and bottom
Front wing: White whitetail deer belly hair
Hackle: Dark brown rooster
Originator: Gary LaFontaine

Hi-Vis Parachute

Hook: Standard Dry TMC 101, sizes #20 to #26
Thread: 8/0 gray
Tail: Grizzly hackle
Body: Beaver or muskrat, gray or black
Post: Hi-Vis, Z-lon, or Antron
Hackle: Grizzly
Originator: Trapper Badovinac

LaFontaine Improved Buzzball

Hook: Standard dry TMC 100, size #14 or #16
Body: Medium dun and orange grizzly hackle. Palmered and trimmed to hook gape.
Overbody: Sized grizzly hackle
Wing: White or clear Antron
Note: This simple fly does a very good job of imitating midges when they cluster.
Originator: Gary LaFontaine

Bucktail Caddis Variant

Hook: 2xl, 2xf – TMC 5212, size #8 or #10
Thread: 8/0 brown
Body: Burnt orange or dark ginger Haretron dubbing
Body hackle: Dark barred ginger, palmered
Underwing: Krystal Flash
Wing: Dark brown bucktail or natural deer hair
Hackle: Dark brown rooster
Originator: Trapper Badovinac

Griffiths Gnat

Hook: Standard dry TMC 100, sizes #16 to #22
Body: Peacock herl
Hackle: Grizzly
Originator: George Griffiths

Many anglers think that if they have slack in their line, they won't be able to set the hook when the fish takes the fly. They don't consider that when the trout takes the fly, there is nothing between them and the fish but air. Aggressive hook sets are counterproductive—simply take the slack out of the line and let the fish help set the hook. If you are used to catching 8" fish, your hook sets can be very hard and you won't often break the tippet because the fish doesn't have enough mass to do that. He'll move with your hook set. On the Missouri, you will catch trout mostly over 15" and some over 20". An aggressive hook set will either break the tippet, straighten the hook, or pull it from the fish's mouth because the trout has so much more mass and moves very little when you initially set the hook. Light hook sets, especially when fishing small dry flies, are what is needed.

Rigging

A two-fly rig is the norm for most anglers here. Tie a 24" butt section onto your fly line and then, with a blood knot, attach a 9' 4X leader to the butt. Loop to loop leaders are convenient, but collapse in the wind. I use the same two-fly set-up for dry flies as I do with nymphs, but add one more option. Thread the 4X tippet through the eye of the top (indicator) fly then, using a blood knot, tie on a 24" to 36" section of 5X. Then tie the dropper fly onto the end of this section of tippet with an improved Clinch knot. This technique will work if you properly match the tippet size to the eye of the top fly. If you try to use too large a fly, the knot will pass through the eye. Most tippets will form a large enough knot to keep the top fly above it, but new fluorocarbons and newly designed hooks with extra large eyes may make this set-up unworkable. Experiment. The great part of this rig is that the top fly can move more freely than one where the tippet is tied off the bend of the hook.

Presentation

Casting directly upstream to risers will often spook them when your fly line hits the water, particularly in slick water. Approaching from the upstream side allows you to show the fish the fly first instead of your fly line, but added stealth is needed on the approach since they will be facing upstream.

A reach cast is a great cast to know on the Missouri and it's merely a slight modification to a conventional forward cast. It's simply taking the tip of your rod and "reaching" it upstream as the fly and the line are extended out over the water on the final delivery. Releasing the fly line as you reach will keep the fly on target. This cast, especially when used with a slightly downstream presentation, effectively mends the line before it touches the water. Longer drag-free drifts are accomplished because the fly is downstream of the line. When fishing from a drift boat, this cast will allow you present the fly drag-free for very long distances.

False casting over fish, especially when they are holding close to the surface, will send them packing. The droplets of water from your line plus the line's overhead movement itself will put them down. Why exactly that spooks them is a guess. Perhaps an osprey delivers water spray just prior to picking up a fish, and the line movement looks like wings.

Slapping the fly to the water doesn't work here, even with hopper patterns. It normally will just send the fish off to safer water. It also drowns the fly as it penetrates the surface film. To remedy this, stop your forward cast higher so that the rod tip doesn't come down close to the water.

Dry Fly Patterns

For dry flies, color is the least important feature. When a trout is looking up into the sunlight at a natural insect, he mostly sees a silhouette. Size and shape are important but color, especially, color within the range, doesn't matter much. Also, if you begin to study the entomology of a stream, you will see color variations even with the same species. And I've read studies that found color variations within a brood.

The thunderstorm is over and the sun returns, forming a double rainbow over Pelican Point.

Catch and Release

To fly fishermen, the word is out that "Catch and Release" is a good idea. Words like "Zero Limit" and TU logos are sewn onto our buddy's vest or stuck to SUV windows. There is a faint memory of Lee Wulff's inspiring words about the fish you catch being a gift from someone who caught it and released it. The image of a bait fisherman proudly displaying a stringer full of fish to his wife is a bit disturbing.

And yet "Zero Limit" doesn't mean "Zero Killed." Good intentions are no substitute for good practice and knowledge. Fly fishing, even when we do everything right, isn't a 100% bloodless sport. Gathering information will help you gain better techniques so that you can minimize the impact on the resource we all share. The phrase "Catch and Release" doesn't usually come with a set of instructions–but in this book it does. And this time the instructions are based on eighteen scientific studies carried out over a sixty-year period, plus the observations of professionals who spend their lives handling fish.

Learning from Studies

As fly fishermen we need to know how we can continue to enjoy our sport without adversely affecting the fish population. By changing a few things we can positively affect the resource.

A frequent question is "Why should I think that any of the fish I catch and release die as a result of my handling?" The short answer is that some of the fish you release will die as a result of your actions even if you do everything correctly. Cal Ripken, Jr., played over 2,600 consecutive baseball games. Was it just luck that he never got injured? Was it genetics? Or maybe the fact that he religiously worked out, even in the off-season, to keep himself in top physical shape had something to do with it. Probably it was all those things together. In the National Football League, the players who play the longest are typically those who have the least amount of physical contact with the other team. There are, of course, exceptions but kickers tend to have longer, more injury-free careers than running backs. We can apply this to fly-fishing for trout–the fish with the least contact with us have the highest chances of living a long life. The fish that is handled without injury will live longer than one that is not.

It seems like each week we hear of a new study linking cancer to anything from bacon to bicycle seats. It doesn't take long for information overload to set in and then we tend to ignore all new information. It raises the question "How can so many studies conflict so much?" The answer is one we already know–the studies are biased. And if you look at only one study you get only one biased outcome. Each study will have data that could be reported differently. For example, we measure the IQ of 100 blue-eyed fourth graders. We don't report each of their scores because we don't like the results we got, so instead we report "More than half of those tested had an IQ higher than average." So the unanswered questions are: 1. Is "more than half" 50.1% or 99.9%? 2. Is "average" of this group alone? Blue-eyed fourth graders in the western U.S.? Or was it measured against fourth graders in general, including developing countries?

The result of one study is more valuable if you combine the results of numerous studies. Matthew J. Taylor and Karl R. White did this in a study titled *A Meta-Analysis of Hooking Mortality of Nonanadromous Trout* (North American Journal of Fisheries Management, 1992). Taylor and White wrote:

"The results of hooking mortality of nonanadromous trout were integrated with meta-analysis. Studies were coded for all variables suspected of having a relationship to rates of hooking mortality. The analysis showed that trout caught on bait died at higher rates than trout caught on artificial flies or lures, that fish caught on barbed hooks had higher mortality rates than fish caught on barbless hooks, that brown trout (*Salmo trutta*) had lower mortality rates than other species of nonanadromous trout, and that wild trout died at higher rates than hatchery-reared trout. Other variables, including size of hooks, number of hooks, and water temperature, did not show a statistically significant relationship to hooking mortality. The results of this review should assist fisheries management agencies in refining and developing policies regarding fisheries regulations."

Barbed versus Barbless

It probably won't amaze anyone that fish caught on baited barbed hooks have a high mortality rate when released. Trout tend to swallow bait much deeper than artificial lures or flies, and trying to remove those barbed hooks from deep within a fish's gullet amounts to surgery and long periods of time out of the water. All 18 of the hooking mortality studies Taylor and White

considered agree that the mortality rate is greater while using bait versus flies, and barbed hooks result in higher mortality than barbless hooks. A baited barbed hook killed 33.5% released fish, while a fly with a single barbless hook killed 2.6%. The mortality rate for flies doubled when anglers used barbed hooks (4.8%) and barbless baited hooks dropped the kill rate to 8.4%.

I know many fly fishermen who insist that they catch more fish with a barbed hook and I won't argue with them. But how would one know? Did they perform a scientific study with a control group over a several-year period or is it just a gut feeling? I have done some quasi-scientific experiments. In 1999, I guided fifty trips on the Missouri River where I had two fly fishermen in my drift boat. In the morning I gave one guy barbed flies and the other barbless. I didn't tell anyone what I was doing. In the afternoon I switched.

Some days the barbed hooks would catch more, some days fewer, but overall it was almost a wash—with the barbless flies landing about 2% more fish. But 100% of the time retrieving the fly from the fish's mouth was easier with the barbless hook. This also translated to a cost savings for me because on my trips I supply the flies, and I have found that the flies themselves take much less of a beating if I don't have to twist them around with a pair of hemostats. The barbless flies often fall out of the fish when it gets into the net, or a slight push of the fly sets it free. Trout caught on barbless hooks take less time to release, probably a factor in their lower mortality rate. I've heard guys say that a de-barbed hook will penetrate deeper and will cause a higher mortality rate. But all the studies I have found contradict this theory. The next time you stick yourself with that barbed #14 Royal Wulff, ask yourself if the tissue damage is the same for barbed versus barbless hooks.

Hooks

The studies revealed no significant difference between single and treble hooks, and also none between hook sizes for the lures and flies. But two things jump out when reviewing this part of the data. The first is that there is a trend toward less mortality when using smaller hooks for the baited hooks. The second is that there were no hooks smaller than a #14 used. The hook sizes ranged from #4s to #14s, but the results don't show which of the killed fish were caught on lures. This study, done on nonanadromous trout, makes me ask how many fly fishermen fish for trout with #4 flies. Maybe it's a matter of style, but my average fly size is probably around a #18. My observation is that you do very little tissue damage to a fish with a de-barbed #22 Trico pattern.

The Trout

Brown trout had the lowest mortality (1%) followed by brook (3.4%), cutthroat (3.5%), rainbow (6.9%), and lake (12.6%). With bait, the mortality was much higher but the order remained the same except for cutthroat (50%) and rainbow (41%). Another part of the analysis found that "the average length of a fish had a significantly positive relationship to hooking mortality; the longer the fish, the higher the mortality." What's unknown is the length of all these samples. If, for example, the length of the lake and rainbow trout were much bigger than the brown trout, it could affect the outcome. The study also found that hatchery trout (3.8% mortality) fared better than wild trout (5.1% mortality). This result came with a disclaimer "...hatchery fish suffered lower hooking mortality rates than wild fish. In the majority of studies with wild trout, the fish were released into some form of artificial holding area (e.g., live-boxes, live sacks), which probably kept them from feeding;

A lone angler works his fly in the cold springtime flow at the Bullpen near Holter Dam.

fasting, along with the altered environment, may have increased the mortality rates for these samples. Most hatchery fish, however, were returned to raceways like those in which they had been reared, and they likely adapted to the feeding regimens during the holding period. Because of these treatment differences, it would be best to consider the wild fish-hatchery fish comparisons with caution."

Pelicans can be fun to watch as they not-so-gracefully fly or swim.
When they land, en masse, on your pod of rising fish they lose their novelty.

Etiquette and Ethics

When my friend Terry Barragree and I, along with our fathers, would pile in to his dad's '51 Chevy pickup and head into the Colorado high country, we really never talked about etiquette. It was a word that I associated with table manners and how burping was something to do quietly. That was the time of Elvis and Buddy Holly, of Chevy Nomad wagons, and of waiting another few years to be fourteen so I could get a deer license. Whenever we fished, etiquette wasn't a consideration because we rarely ever saw anyone else on the river.

Other times, Terry and I would ride our bikes down to the Arkansas River and catch hatchery trout that we called stockers. The only person we ever saw was an old black man who asked us to keep any suckers we caught for him. Sure, sometimes we would get frisky and one would pitch a flat stone into a beaver pond that the other guy was fishing. Then the thrower would see a stick or rock come flying back his way, but usually we would just leap frog each other up or down a stretch of water as we filled our creels with fish and wet grass to keep them fresh. We fished until we caught our limit and then headed home, or sometimes we caught grasshoppers and pitched them into the river to watch the browns crash on the squirming chunks. There were no crowds, no drift boats, and few other fishermen.

He and I still fish together, but now he's Griz and I'm Trapper and etiquette is a term that we do think of while fly fishing.

I typically average about 100 days of guiding each year. Normally I have two clients each day. After you guide even five or so years you end up sharing a day with a lot of different people. After five years you tend to see people you recognize but strain to remember their names. After a short but awkward meeting and exchange of names, you begin to recall them by one incident or another. "Remember that fish we chased down river for almost a mile? Man that was a big brown." Then everything comes back to you. It's rare that the memory you have of someone is a negative one. Fly fishermen are just good people. The exceptions are so few they are statistically irrelevant. Some guys are better at nymphing than others. Some choose to only cast to rising fish. Others want to improve a technique, and almost all are open to learning something new. It's rare that it's only about catching fish.

I met my clients in Ovando. We had fished the Missouri for a few days and they wanted to try something a little different. It was early fall and there was frost on the tubes of my Avon raft. We launched on the North Fork of the Blackfoot, and Bob and

Tom were in awe of just how crystal clear the water was. The North Fork runs pretty low in the fall so we floated through, occasionally getting out to pull the raft over gravel bars. We hit River Junction that put us on the main stem of the Blackfoot River. We weren't seeing much of a hatch but the view was spectacular. We saw bald eagles and deer along the river's bank. Switching over to Wooly Buggers was the ticket. We landed several nice browns, rainbows, and cutthroat before the action stopped as quickly as it started.

The October Caddis hatch started with just a few, but by the time we pulled over and changed over to floating lines and the big dries, it was in full force. Risers were coming up to sample the big flies and we were anxious to try our imitations. It seemed like even the sloppy presentations were going to hook fish as they attacked the orange Bucktail Caddis and the Lovebug dropper. Some of the fish we were taking were pretty small, but Bob and Tom were having the time of their lives. Neither had ever seen an October Caddis before and we stopped a couple of times to capture some to examine.

Bob hooked up a small rainbow and watched as the little eight-inch fish leaped and ran like it was being pursued by a demon. It was. "Trapper, what's the story with this fish?" he asked.

"Oh, man. Bob, hang on, you are about to see something really amazing," I replied. I didn't have time to explain and figured it was best he experience it for himself. Suddenly his rod bent with a newly acquired heavy load.

"Trapper, I'm hung up on something." He turned to the side of the raft, as the load on the other end started moving upstream.

"Hang on Bob. Play it like it's a big fish. You aren't hung up, you've got a bulltrout on." After a couple of minutes we finally got to see the mystery. I had the net ready and as Bob played the fish up to the boat he saw nature at work. A 2-pound bulltrout had the little rainbow sideways in his mouth. He had seen the fish in distress and did what predators have done for eons—he attacked. I reached under both fish trying to get him in the net, but the bulltrout slipped off into the deeper water and disap-

peared. I turned to Bob who was having a hard time believing what he just saw, when suddenly the bulltrout came up again and grabbed the stunned rainbow for the second time. I tried to net him again, and again he slipped off into the deeper water. I then decided that the poor rainbow had probably been through enough so after reviving him, I released it wondering if this mountain lion with fins was waiting for his prey in the shadows.

Bob and Tom stood on the bank for well over fifteen minutes talking about what had just happened. Neither had ever seen a bulltrout and this was something beyond what they ever imagined.

"Did you see him come back the second time?" They kept asking each other the same question over and over. It was fun to watch them be so blown away. As we were getting back in the boat, Tom turned to me and said, "You know. This was worth the entire trip to Montana. You've given me a gift that I can keep forever and I really want to thank you." Bob chimed in with similar accolades and gratitude. It was a bonding experience, and I was glad to be part of it.

Neither one of these men was concerned that we didn't even land the bulltrout. Neither of them cared the least about the small fish they caught. They were just two guys out in a raft with a guide having fun. We didn't catch a record number of fish that day, and most of the ones we did catch were much smaller than the hogs on the Missouri.

Paradoxically, fly fishing isn't about catching fish.

Unwritten Rules

In many sports there are absolute rules about what is too close. In football, if you tackle a receiver before the ball gets to him, your entire team is penalized and you get to look stupid while knowing everyone is questioning your proficiency. In basketball, if you grab the arm of a player as he's about to shoot a lay-up, the ref will blow the whistle and point at you and then send your opponent to the free-throw line. In fly fishing, there are no play clocks or referees. There isn't even a set of rules that you can read. How close is too close to another fisherman? The answer is a great big "It depends."

I used to hear that a good rule of thumb was to fish "out of sight" of other fishermen. But here in Montana, because you can sometimes see downriver for a mile or so, that would mean only about twenty-five people at one time could fish the Missouri River between Holter Dam and the Cascade Bridge. I think it's unreasonable, especially during the peak seasons, to follow this visual rule of thumb. If you are fishing a big river that you can't wade across, why not fish the other side of the river from someone else?

But the other end of the scale needs study also. If you are fishing a river in winter, as my brother Dan and I were a couple of years ago, and there isn't another fisherman for miles, why would you walk between two brothers who weren't more than 50 feet apart and start fishing? When this happened to us, we each thought it was some sort of practical joke. I kept thinking this guy was someone I knew and he was suddenly going to look up and start laughing his ass off, and then my brother and I would start laughing. But we didn't know him and we weren't amused. I didn't want to hear his story about how this was "his spot." I just wanted to get away from him. This is the type of incident that

To be the only angler on any stretch of river means you have to fish the places that everyone else ignores or get up early or fish late.

97

This single-lane bridge at the town of Craig will soon be gone.
Taking turns crossing this bridge seems foreign to some.

that they fly fish because they're hungry. And, since most of us practice Catch and Release techniques, there is no way to really keep score. Besides, it's not a contest to see who can catch the most fish. The quality of a day of fishing isn't measured by the number of fish caught any more than the quality of a day of skiing is measured by how many runs you made.

The Missouri River has a large trout population, but they are not just in one place. You will find an ample number of trout on every section of the river between Holter Dam and the Cascade Bridge. If you encounter another angler who is catching fish after fish, it's not because he's found the only honey hole on the river, it's because he's skilled. He's figured out what the trout are eating, selected the right fly, and made the correct presentation. Crowding him is going to turn his experience sour and make you look like a moron.

While it's tough to give an exact distance, I would say that, if you are upstream of this angler, the end of your line at the end of the drift should never be closer than 100 feet to him. If you take all the fly line off your reel and add another 15 feet, you'll be pretty close to 100 feet. But instead of seeing how close you can come to another angler without pissing him off, a more reasonable solution is to go somewhere else. If you are driving down the road looking for a place to fish, stop at a place where there aren't a lot of people. Once upon a time, someone fishing away from the crowd discovered each and every honey hole on every river in the United States. The crowds formed after these discoveries were made. And, as water conditions move gravel bars and fishing traffic pressures fish to move,

sometimes end in fist fights or heated exchanges of four-letter words.

Different fly fishermen have different reasons to fish. Some do it because they are learning and would like to get better at it. Some like being away from phones, faxes, and work. Some enjoy being outside with the opportunity to have a close encounter with those things wild and untamed. I've yet to hear anyone say

Fly fishing is a captivating sport because trout tend to inhabit water that is clean, cold, and running through some really pretty country.

the best fishing spots will change. Discovering these newly formed pockets where fish concentrate is a wonderful thrill. It probably won't stay a secret for long, but you will always have that blissful memory of discovery.

If you find yourself in your newfound sweet spot, serenely casting to and catching a seemingly endless number of trout, and your success is noticed by others who have decided to join you, what do you do? What is your response if two anglers box you in while they continue to move closer and closer?

Here in Montana, oftentimes the original angler will ask the interlopers, "Where are you from?" This act of crowding is mostly foreign to residents, so they assume that the answer is going to be outside the state. And even though it sounds like an innocuous question, it's really just a polite way of asking, "Is everyone from your state a rude bastard like you?"

To crowd someone out of a spot is the truest sign of an immature angler. It speaks volumes about you without a word being spoken. This is the equivalent of tailgating someone at 75 mph on an empty highway. It's a threat and a challenge, and I've seen it turn ugly. If you fly fish for the serenity of it, why would you provoke a confrontation?

Opinions vary, but mine is that fly fishing has nothing to do with numbers of fish caught. Long after you've forgotten how many fish you caught in one day, you'll remember those special ones. Maybe it's that one fish that was feeding in a very tough-to-get-to spot. Or the one that leaped in the air, eye level with you, and then threw the fly. The one that got you into your backing so fast, you were happy you weren't standing on your line because it would have launched you into the river. But when fly fishers recall bad days on the river, it always seems to involve someone being rude—conflict doesn't make for a great day of fishing. Fly fishing is not a competitive sport. The guy with the most fish at the end of the day doesn't win anything. It's like counting the number of dates you've gone on in your life. You won't remember how many, but you will remember the special ones.

How long should you occupy a particular sweet stretch of river? If there were no others in sight, I would say as long as you wish. If others approach and you've had a great time, the relevant question to ask yourself is "Would catching one more fish make the difference between a good and bad day?" If the answer is "No," then be graceful and move on, or sit and enjoy while others share the fun that results from your generosity. You'd be surprised at how quickly you can make lifelong friends out of total strangers this way. You will quickly realize the true joy of fly fishing and of being a genuine gentleman.

Dogs

While fly fishing, it is my experience that a well trained dog is a joy, and an unruly dog is a pain in the ass. Many breeds of dogs have a deep-seated instinct to retrieve anything you throw into the water, including a #16 Elk Hair caddis. If your dog tries to retrieve your fly, he's likely going to swim through the pod of fish you are trying to catch. If he tries to retrieve another angler's fly or wants to play with other fisherman, you probably won't be one of the most popular people on the river.

Many dogs also love to bark at everything that moves. If you find yourself being barked at for the act of casting, the only thing more annoying than the hours of barking is when the dog decides to swim out to the island you are fishing off, then gets swept away in the current and swims through your pod of rising fish. The most ardent of dog lovers is going to frown on this action.

Watching a well trained bird dog work a field is a thing of beauty. A trained retriever that will swim into water only a few degrees from being ice, to get the goose or duck you shot, is a valuable companion and friend. I've observed these animals sitting patiently in a boat until commanded to go to work. I absolutely love this kind of dog. They ignore everything except their owner. They don't bark unless there is reason to and they don't pace from one end of the boat to the other. The owners of these animals have spent hours working with them and the payoff is a dog that everyone can enjoy. A well trained dog is a mag-

If solitary fly fishing is what you seek, try fishing the seasons when others are staying home.

nificent sight. An untrained dog should be left at home.

Floating Etiquette

When wade fishing you should consider distances to other anglers, and when floating give the same consideration. On all rivers in Montana there are regulations regarding just how close a boat may legally get to swimmers, divers, and wading anglers. While these regulations change, and it's a good idea to check, the legal distance is currently 75' from wading anglers or roughly the length of your entire fly line. There are exceptions to this rule. If you find yourself floating down a narrow side channel and, as you go around a tight corner, you discover a wading angler, there is little you can do but apologize, but do that, then pull in your line and wait until you are well past him. Your boat floating over his feeding fish isn't going to make him happy. Casting to his rising fish is akin to going into his backyard and slapping his kids. If the situation is such that you can't stay far enough away to avoid drifting through his water, and if there is enough room

Float fishing etiquette is more just common sense. When you see anglers wading downstream, move to another part of the river.

behind him with enough water, float behind the angler after announcing your intentions.

Whenever you overtake a slower downstream boat, be sure to give them the same 75' or more when you drift by. Watch downstream floaters to try to determine what they are doing. If they seem to be methodically working a particular bank, don't race around them and cut in just downstream. Instead, fish the other bank, hold back, or drop anchor until they are approximately twenty to thirty minutes ahead of you and then fish their bank, or push downstream to gain that twenty- to thirty-minute buffer between you and them.

It's not uncommon for the Missouri River to produce summertime "air mattress hatches." These leisure floaters are often equipped with high-powered water cannons, and most will return fire on your boat if you initiate a salvo of your own. Keep in mind that if their upstream companions see this exchange, they will regard you as a pirate ship and fire on you as they float by.

By and large, the leisure floaters stick to the middle of the river where the current is strongest, so close encounters are minimal. Sometimes, inexperienced floaters will unknowingly drift right through your pod of gulpers. Trying to give an entomology lecture to these floaters is a waste of time, although sometimes jokingly demanding a beer for their trespass can garner you a nice mid-afternoon refreshment. While most don't understand the nuances of fly fishing, they are aware enough to know that their presence can disrupt your day, so most make great effort to avoid contact but occasionally it happens. When that happens, take it in stride, and remember that they have chosen some simple old-fashioned fun instead of the destructive things that others their age may be engaged in.

Montana has chosen to name their boat launches Fishing Access Sites, or "FAS." When this name appears on maps or fishing literature, it's almost an invitation to set up a lawn chair there. If you are trying to launch a boat or raft with a ramp full of kids playing tag while Dad fishes, it can be frustrating. Talk to them. Explain that you will launch your boat and be out of their

way in minutes. When you are backing down the ramp, have a friend get behind the trailer to direct you and to ensure that no harm is done to children or adults.

When you drive to an FAS, park your rig away from the ramp and prepare yourself and boat for launching. If you have a raft, move it out of the way to inflate it so that others can launch while you are preparing. It should only take a few minutes to get your boat in and your rig off the ramp. If you are new to backing up trailers, practice at home or in an empty parking lot so that you won't embarrass yourself by "chasing your trailer" or damaging someone else's boat. The same is true at the take-out–get your boat out and move away from the ramp to prepare your boat for towing.

Litter

Don't do it. The river is not a garbage can. Fish and birds shouldn't or won't eat the rest of your lunch or snack. Beer cans and bottles will still be in the river long after you are dead and buried. If you don't want to look at your trash, just think what the guy who finds it will think. Make every attempt to retrieve anything that blows out or falls out of your boat or vest.

Why Fish?

Catch and Release methods have saved us from having to settle for fishing for small hatchery fish, but there is mortality even under the best of conditions. If you carefully study and practice the proper methods, you will greatly reduce your impact on fish populations–but it won't ever be zero.

Reading the chapter entitled Catch and Release is a good start, but the easiest way to quickly cut the mortality rates is to smash your barbs. Then consider limiting the number of fish you hook. If you don't hook a fish, you won't hurt it. I stand with many others who have made a conscious decision to challenge what we know about fly fishing.

Several years ago I gave my brother a copy of a photo I took of him with a really nice rainbow. He was holding the fish in front of him and smiling at the camera. I thought he would appreciate this captured moment.

"What's this?" he asked.

"A fishing photo."

"I already have this one."

"No, you don't. I just took this last week."

"Yes, I do."

What it made me realize is that after a while they all look alike; same hat, same vest, same fly rod, same waders, even the same happy smile.

Most fly fishers have a favorite photo of a fishing trip. Photos are a great way to preserve the experience without harming the fish. Some fly fishers take a photo of every fish caught and my guess is they think the lab has made multiple prints of the same shot just as my brother did.

How much harm it does to the fish depends on you. I've seen guys play a fish for way longer than they should have and then strangle it in a nylon net while they fumbled to get their camera out of their bag. A buddy, unfamiliar with the camera, needed several moments to set the camera aperature or just to find the shutter button, all while the angler with the fish is holding the fish out of the water, often over the boat or shore, smiling at the camera, and saying, "Take the picture." Then another buddy says, "Here, take one with my camera." And the process continues. Then, when the Kodak moments are finished, they either toss the fish nonchalantly into the water, or make only minimal attempts at reviving it.

I once asked a guy who treated a fish in this manner why he thought the fish would live. He said, "Hey, he swam away."

I said, "Yes, he did. I've also shot bull elk through the heart with a 180-grain bullet and watched them run over a hill. When I tracked them they were dead. Just because I didn't see them die doesn't mean they weren't dead."

While many anglers show a great deal of pride from catching a large trout, few call their buddies over to see the 6" rainbows

in their net. Instead they treat them like nuisances, casually throwing them over their shoulders or bouncing them off the boat bottom. But, where do big trout come from? The Missouri is a wild trout fishery, so you won't see a hatchery truck dumping thousands of fish at one of the boat ramps. If you mistreat or kill the small fish, especially with the ongoing fight against whirling disease, you will have your own answer a few years from now to the question "Where are all the big fish?"

Respect the resource. Someone else likely treated your fish well so that you could catch him. Return the favor to the next guy.

If I am having a hell of a day catching fish on nymphs, I like to try different dry attractor patterns to see if I can get them to come up for my fly when they obviously prefer feeding on the bottom. If I'm catching one fish after another on hoppers, I sometimes break the hook at the bend. I have the thrill of watching a fish take my pattern without having to bring it to the net. This is especially rewarding when your arm and ligaments are sore.

My philosophy is that when we are getting the trout to hit a particular pattern on most casts, it becomes redundant to keep doing it. Much of the fun of fly fishing is derived from finding out what stage of a hatch they are feeding on and then finding what's in your box that will best imitate it. Then, after you've caught a number of fish, it's just a matter of doing it over and over again unless you change the rules.

Many have questioned my sanity when I catch a few fish on a pattern and then change flies. This is how I discover new patterns. Once you know they are actively feeding, showing them your new pattern is very telling. This is also the best time to try that new method you read about in a book or magazine. If you try the method when nothing else has worked and it fails too, you still don't know whether it's the technique or the fish just aren't in the mood. Trying this new method when you know the fish are actively feeding will tell you much about the technique or how well you are doing what the author suggested.

And then there may be a time in your day when you just say you've caught enough fish, when you want to savor what you've experienced instead of focusing on catching another fish. This may also be the time to put down your rod and help a friend who is struggling with gear or technique and getting frustrated watching you pull in so many when he can't even catch one. The paradox is that fly fishing doesn't have to be about catching fish.

When you find a particular hot spot, enjoy it and then move on so that others can share the fun that you experienced. The boat just upstream may hold a beginner who is about to catch their first trout on a fly rod, or maybe an aging gentleman who is about to catch his last.

Whirling Disease

This disease, caused by a parasitic protozoan has been seen in many Montana rivers. Affecting fish's brains, whirling disease causes the creatures to become unbalanced and swim in circles, thus the name. Fishermen can spread the parasites when they travel from one fishery to another if they don't take the time to properly clean their waders and boots, as well as boats, rafts, and pontoons. Anything that makes contact with the water can carry the disease. Take the time to wash your gear. There are new products being developed that will kill the spores that cause the infection, but you have to buy them and use them. Because research is ongoing, the best source for current information is www.whirling-disease.org/

Whirling disease can kill large numbers of small fish. Taking the time to clean your gear is a way to help.

*Nice warm sunny days are plentiful during a Montana summertime,
but being prepared for sudden changes will allow you to fish in comfort.*

Weather, Clothing, and Gear

Weather

I've lived in the Rocky Mountains for most of my life. I spend much of my time outdoors in all kinds of winter. I've seen it snow in July and I've seen 70° Fahrenheit in January. Normal is not a word that people in Montana use to describe the weather. The weather guys can record temperature and precipitation over a period of years and let you know what average is, but they can't define normal.

When I was a kid in Colorado I used to wear hip boots and jeans most of the time while fishing. Then I graduated to rubber Red Ball waders that mostly kept me dry, but then I walked and felt like those knights in armor—only without the beautiful princess.

When neoprene waders came along I thought my prayers had been answered. But, while they worked better than anything I had ever used, they were still torture in summer and clammy in winter.

Then, somewhere in the distance I heard the sound of trumpets, and the clouds parted and revealed Gore-Tex® and Polar fleece. I'm sure that some time in the future a new material will be developed that far surpasses what we have now. But when I think back to the cotton, waffle-weave long johns I used to wear and all the days I spent shivering, I'm happy to enjoy the comforts of the new materials that just keep getting better every year.

I guided a couple of guys from Florida one year. It was late September and, when I arrived at the shop to meet them, it was snowing at a rate of 3" an hour, and the thermometer was stuck at 25°. They brought shorts and light jackets and told me "When we were here last year, it was almost ninety degrees." I explained to them that the day before it had been in the 70s and sunny. In the early 1990s we had 6" of snow in the middle of August in Craig. It can be 90° one day and 45° the next.

Montana is a place of extremes. If you are prepared for those extremes, it can be exhilarating. If you are not prepared it's just plain miserable.

Layers

In general, visitors to Montana should bring clothing for all weather conditions from scorching hot to freezing cold. Layering your clothing, when done correctly, is going to keep you comfortable. But many people have only a vague idea about what that means and don't consider that the type of layer is equally important.

Many manufacturers have jumped on the bandwagon for synthetic outdoor clothing. Take some time to study and then buy what fits your needs and your budget. I've guided hundreds of fishermen. I've seen healthy adult men go hypothermic in a matter of an hour wearing jeans and hip boots in rainy weather. Nothing takes the fun out of fly fishing faster than being cold and wet, and often the very best fishing is when the weather is cold and wet.

Cotton Sabotage

If the weather turns nasty, keeping your skin dry and warm is the name of the game. Basically, that means that the layer you have next to your skin has to be of a material that will wick away moisture and move it to the next layer. That material is not cotton.

Cotton is a wonderful product. It's cool and comfortable and is great stuff while you're sitting in a bar drinking beer at the end of the day. It's not very functional as outdoor clothing. When the weather is hot and sunny, cotton still isn't the best choice. Cotton T-shirts will stretch and you can easily burn through the porous weave. When cotton gets wet, it takes a long time to dry. If you happen to find yourself in the middle of a mosquito hatch they will see your body as a Happy Meal. Modern materials like Supplex protect your skin against the sun, dry quickly, and have a weave tight enough to discourage insect bites.

You also don't want to sabotage your layering system by putting a layer of cotton on next to your skin. If you are planning to fish in Montana, especially in those transitional months of March through May and again in September through November, invest in some Capilene® or equivalent underwear. There are several manufacturers out there making this type of synthetic base layer. It doesn't make sense to buy all the other layers and then wear cotton briefs and a cotton T-shirt because any moisture on your skin will be absorbed and held by this material instead of pass-

ing it on to move it away from your skin. Even if it's not raining or snowing this is important, because if you are warm and you step into cold water, you are going to get condensation. Being clammy all day is uncomfortable and if the temperature drops, clammy can quickly turn to dismal.

The Thermal Layer

My brothers Tom and Mark never seemed to pick up our dad's love of fishing. That was left to my brother Dan and me, who still fish together because he is also my next door neighbor. We seldom were very competitive about it, but when we were younger he had the size factor in his favor, being six years older.

I got up early one morning while we were summer camping, to be the first one to the water. There was a small wooden dock on this lake within a stone's throw of our tent, and it was just wide enough for one adult man but offered plenty of room for a scrawny seven-year-old. I was filling the stringer up at a record pace when Dan finally stumbled out of the wall tent. The morning air was cool and the lake held a wavering mist close to its glassy surface. The only disturbance was my constant landing of fish. Seeing this he quickly grabbed his gear and headed for the dock.

What he didn't know but soon discovered was that the fish were crowded around the very end of the dock and casts anywhere else went unanswered. He tried casting around me but I deferred his attempts by throwing a strategic hip at the right time. He kept trying to reason with me to share the wealth, but I wasn't having any part of it. I had found the mother lode and I wasn't about to share it with anyone, including my own brother.

His moment in fishing infamy happened when I ran out of night crawlers and had to go back to the end of the dock to replenish my bait can. He seized the moment and commandeered the prized spot on the end of the dock, using my same tactics to keep me at bay. I was no match for him as he was twice my size. Now Dan has always been a happy guy—quick to laugh and the first in line for anything fun. He was razzing me to no

Unless you show up in mid-winter, you're not likely to see a great deal of snow and ice,
but dressing properly will make the day more enjoyable any time of year.

end while he caught the fish and I had gone from king to pauper in seconds. I pleaded with him to share or at least take turns, but he wasn't about to relinquish the spot. There were no alternatives left. I backed up a few steps, then charged forward, ramming him from the back, sending him flying off the end of the dock and landing spread-eagled with a splash big enough to scare fish on the other side of the lake, but I got my spot back.

Even soaking wet and surprised he came up laughing. His only concern was his wallet. Yes, he is that wonderful of a brother.

Even though this was summertime, he was cold in seconds. Our bodies lose heat fifteen times faster in water, and wet skin cools quickly. You don't have to fall in the water to get cold. Staying dry and having the right clothing is the key to fishing in comfort.

The next layer when it's cold is the thermal layer. This is what will keep you warm and insulate you against cold air or, while you're wade fishing, water. How cold it is will dictate what this layer is composed of. Fleece is a great product. It wicks away moisture from your skin, it's lightweight and it's, well, comfy. There are usually three different weights for most of these materials. So you can buy a weight that suits your activity, but keep in mind that companies like Patagonia design their heaviest fleece for very cold temperatures. While they will wick away the perspiration if you get too warm, it's only within a range. I like their heaviest, "expedition," weight in the winter when the daytime highs aren't getting above freezing and the water temperatures are in the 30s. But most people tell me that I'm crazy when it comes to being willing to go out in cold weather.

You can add another layer of fleece like a pullover shirt or jacket, and that's great if there is no wind. Wind goes right through most of this stuff unless you buy a product that has a liner, but the easiest solution is to make the top layer a Gore-Tex raincoat and Gore-Tex waders. The raincoats designed for fishing are shorter and typically have large pockets in the front for stowing fly boxes or gloves. They compress into a small parcel

when not in use. The good ones have taped seams and are expensive, but worth their weight in gold when the weather is bad and you are secure and warm inside this protective shell. Rubber raincoats or ponchos are not nearly as functional. Rubber traps any moisture inside. Gore-Tex allows the moisture to escape while keeping the rain out. No, I still don't understand it completely but, after wearing it for a number of years, I can tell you that it does work. I don't understand how someone can draw three-dimensional pictures on a computer, either.

Wool is also a great material. It's warm even when wet but it's also bulky and heavy and, when it's wet, it's really bulky and heavy. And it doesn't seem to have the wicking properties of the synthetics. The one exception is a product called Smartwool®, which is only part wool and part synthetic—great stuff. While they're a little bulkier than fleece, socks made from this fabric are really warm.

The Weather-Stop Layer

The last layer is the one that protects you against the elements of rain and/or wind. Fleece is a remarkable material but if it's raining hard and you don't have a means of keeping that moisture off your body, you will get cold. A good Gore-Tex jacket with a hood is my choice for upper body. Keep in mind that some Gore-Tex raincoats are meant for warmer temperatures and very light rain. If you're out in an all-day rain mixed with sleet and snow, it's a nasty feeling when the jacket leaks at the seams and a miniature water fall cascades down your back and eddies at your underwear.

Waders and Boots

Your waders will take care of your lower body. I've quit wearing my neoprene waders, even in the wintertime. With proper layering, Gore-Tex waders are the best way to move any moisture, whether it's sweat, condensation, or rain from your skin. They also allow you freedom of movement, which is especially important if you are getting in and out of a boat all day with knees that seemed to have worked much better when you were in high school.

Gore-Tex waders breathe, so, while you need extra layers under them, they will keep you more comfortable than neoprene. The temperatures can drop, the wind can come up, and if you are not prepared you'll end up looking like a shaking Popsicle as you trudge back to your truck.

Wade fishers will find that, on the Missouri, felt boots are enough because the river is free of algae and doesn't have a slippery bottom. You won't need studded boots here.

Essentials—Not Accessories

Gloves and a hat balance out the ensemble and you are ready.

Fly fishing gloves get wet as you handle the fly line. Fleece gloves seem to hold the warmth next to your skin better than wool gloves. If you want your hands to be warm all day, bring more than one pair with you.

You may also want to take more than one hat—the right one for conditions. Cotton baseball hats are nice to keep the sun off your face, but if the tops of your ears have seen too many sunny days, you might want to get a hat with a wider brim. It's cheaper than paying a dermatologist to tell you things you already know. Keep in mind that you can always use the hood on your raincoat to keep the moisture off your hat and the back of your neck, but a cotton hat will wick the moisture from the bill to your scalp.

Wool felt hats with wide brims and stampede straps to tie under your chin when it's windy work well. While they can get very warm during the hottest days of summer, you can dip them into the river for a great refresher. For very cold days, you can choose fleece hats that cover your ears—some of them even have bills.

If you are cold in this gear it's probably prudent to stay home and catch up on reading all those fly fishing magazines that have stacked up on your desk. Of course most days during the mid-

dle of the summer won't be cold and these layers of clothing will likely stay in the car or dry box of the boat, and in many cases in the motel room. But, it can and does snow in Montana every month of the year and if you walk out of your cabin with shorts and sandals to find six inches of snow, you'll be happy that you can dig through your bag for some warmer clothes.

The finishing "layer" is vital to protecting your eyes from the rays of the sun, the wind, and errant hooks. Polarized sunglasses can allow you to see fish below the surface as well as that log you are about to trip over. If you are fishing out of a boat, consider the wraparound or side-shield styles to protect you from flying hooks—your own as well as the other angler's.

Pack It All

Always remember that Montana holds the official record for 24-hour temperature change—100°! It went from +55° to -45° below in one day. Be prepared for anything. But even when you are dressed correctly you'll still likely get cold hands and feet. Wading a river with water temperatures in the 40s can be tricky when numb feet make moving around seem about as natural as driving a car with swim fins on your feet and hands. A dip in the river is going to shorten your day and may make you wish you had gone to work.

In many places in the world the summers are very hot and very humid. When it clouds up and rains, it just gets more humid and stays hot. Montana has a semi-arid climate that, while it can get up to 100°, is rarely humid. Rain may raise the humidity a bit, but the temperature can plummet. And when the cell or system passes, there is often wind behind. What happens is that you are enjoying a very warm sunny day with temperatures in the 80s. A system moves in, dumps a lot of rain (and sometimes hail) in a short time, then when it stops, you are left standing, soaking wet, in 15 mph wind with the temperature in the 60s and dropping.

If you came prepared you are now in the process of shedding

*Summertime temperatures can reach 100° and protecting your skin
from the sun can be equally as important as protecting it from the cold.*

some of the clothing you donned when it started raining. If you didn't come prepared you are now shivering and doing a wonderful imitation of a snowman without the smile. It all goes back to your own body metabolism and what you packed for the trip. Some people just can't take as much cold as others. I can function pretty well at -30°, but start to wilt when the mercury gets close to 100°.

Equipment

When the question of what equipment is best suited for the Missouri River comes up, the answer will often depend on whose shop you're standing in at the time.

The Blue Ribbon section of the Missouri River between Holter Dam and the town of Cascade runs basically south to north and roughly parallels the Rocky Mountain Front. This is perfectly designed for wind, and there will be many days on the river where wind will be a factor. Add in the big angry fish factor, large water and an often-formidable current, and it spells the need for a rod with some backbone while nymphing. A fast- or medium-fast action rod is your friend here and since there are very few treed banks, a longer rod in the 9' to 9½' range can be used to aid in casting and mending. A Sage XP is a great rod for this river in a 9' to 9½', 6-weight for most situations. A 4- or 5-weight 9' slower-action rod like a Sage SP is a good choice for smaller dry flies or calm days. Many of the Winston and Gary Loomis rods are also excellent choices.

Reels without a good drag will overspool or put you into your backing on every hook up. This is hard on the fish and hard on your arm. The many good brands of reels out there–including Abel, Ross, Galvin, Lamson, and Sage–are lifetime friends.

Finding a place to stay is sometimes the first challenge you will face on your trip. The beauty of the peak times of summer entice many anglers so lodging often books up months in advance.

Shops, Guides, Lodging, and Restaurants

Lodging

In the 35-mile corridor of the Missouri River from Holter Dam to the town of Cascade, there are a few small towns, but none large enough to support a major chain hotel. Despite that fact, there are a surprising number of very good places to stay. Some of these establishments have been around for many years and will no doubt be around for many more.

Keep in mind that lodging along this stretch of Blue Ribbon river fills up months ahead of time during peak summer months. If you drive up to a lodge and ask for a room in July, don't be surprised if the proprietor looks like he's trying to stifle hysterical laughter. All is not lost, however, as you will likely be able to find accommodations in Helena or Great Falls, but these are about 50 miles away. On an average year the rooms within a 15-mile radius of Craig are spoken for early. "Early" means that if you want to stay close to the river in July, you will need to make reservations by Labor Day the previous year.

The following is a partial list. Outfitters and the shops find new accommodations every year, so it's also good to check with them.

Blacktail Ranch

15 MILES WEST OF WOLF CREEK—(406) 235-4330

A full service guest ranch with horseback riding tours. Several different types of cabins are available, and the lodge offers a hot tub and sauna. Meals are available. Rates depend on services you use.

Bungalow Bed and Breakfast

4 MILES WEST OF WOLF CREEK—(406) 235-4276

A historic log home tucked away from the noise of late-night fly fishermen, in a peaceful setting shaded by cottonwoods. There are only four rooms in this quaint home. Meals are available.

End of the Line Sportsmen's Retreat

3 MILES NORTH OF CRAIG—(406) 468-9111 or (406) 443-5220

These two comfortable cottages sit on the banks of the Missouri River and have two bedrooms and two baths each, plus full kitchens and dining areas for you to cook the meals of your choice.

Flyway Ranch

2 MILES SOUTH OF CRAIG—(406) 235-4116

This lodge was converted from a dairy barn, but you would never know from its wonderful decor. The four rooms each have their own baths, and a continental breakfast is part of the room fee. A kitchen and dining room area are available for guests to do their own cooking.

Holter Lake Lodge

2.5 MILES FROM WOLF CREEK BRIDGE—(406) 235-4331

Overlooking Holter Lake, you'll find twelve motel units, each with private bath. There is also a four-bedroom apartment. The dining room is open for all meals.

Missouri River Lodge

2 MILES NORTH OF CRAIG—(406) 468-2224

This log lodge is a stone's throw from the river. It has six bedrooms and bathrooms. Breakfast and dinner are available.

Missouri River Trout Shop and Lodge

CRAIG—(406) 235-4474

The lodge, which is only about 40 yards from the river, has seven rooms, some with private baths plus a café that serves meals including late-night suppers for late-fishing anglers. The rooms are clean and comfortable.

Montana River Outfitters

WOLF CREEK—(800) 800-8218

Seven rustic cabins and four motel rooms, each with its own bathroom. While there is no food service, the town of Wolf Creek has two restaurants.

Sentinel Rock Ranch

1 MILE NORTH OF WOLF CREEK—(406) 235-4474

A converted ranch house, one mile from the river. In addition to a full kitchen, it has four bedrooms and two baths, plus a hot tub.

Wolf Creek Lodge

1 MILE NORTH OF WOLF CREEK—(406) 235-4474

Overlooking the river, this lodge is first class. Its three bedrooms and two baths are elegant. The other amenities include hot tub, steam shower, Jacuzzi, fly-tying room, and a full-sized kitchen and dining area.

Restaurants

While there are plenty of restaurants in Helena and Great Falls, they are fifty miles away. There are a few restaurants in the town of Cascade, about 25 miles north of Craig. But in the immediate area where you'll be fishing the Missouri River, there are about six. Some lodges provide meals for guests but most do not, although many have kitchen facilities available.

Only one service is available to cook for you: Earth to Table, in Craig, (406) 235-9055.

While some places offer box lunches, if you are being guided, that is normally taken care of.

Buying your own food involves making a trip to Cascade or visiting the only local grocery store, at the Exxon Station in Wolf Creek. Or you might want to purchase groceries as you go through Helena or Great Falls on the way to the river.

Fortunately, the eateries around this stretch of the Missouri open early for breakfast, and most stay open late for supper to serve anglers. You will likely hear the adventures of others as you eat dinner or just sit and enjoy a beer or glass of wine. If you are fishing early or late in the season you might find that some of these places have shorter hours than in the summer months. All of these places serve beer and wine and some have full liquor licenses and can sell mixed drinks.

Missouri River Trout Shop Café—(CRAIG)

Hookers Bar & Grill—(CRAIG)

Holter Lake Lodge—(ON HOLTER LAKE)

The Frenchman and Me—(WOLF CREEK)

The Oasis—(WOLF CREEK)

Osterman's Missouri River Inn—(HARDY)

Shops

Missouri River Trout Shop
CRAIG—(406) 235-4474

This is a full-service specialty fly shop with a full line of rods, reels, flies, and gear. Boat rentals and shuttle service are available, as well as guide service.

Montana River Outfitters
WOLF CREEK—(800) 800-8218

Flies and some gear are available at this shop, as are guide and shuttle services.

Cross Currents
(406) 235-3433 Craig, (406) 449-2292 Helena

This Orvis shop is at two locations—one full-service specialty shop in downtown Helena, and the satellite shop in Craig. Both offer rods, reels, flies, and gear, but the shop in Craig is much smaller. They will also take care of your boat rentals, shuttling, and guide service.

Terminal Tackle
WOLF CREEK—(406) 235-9000

A small but enthusiastic shop offering flies, gear, guides, shuttle service, and boat rentals.

Outfitters and Guides

Hiring a guide to introduce you to the current mood of the river is a good idea. I am biased. I am a guide. I've guided many people who spent most of their vacation out here trying to figure out how to catch these fish. Then, on their last day they hired me, unraveled many of their unsolved mysteries, had a great time, and left the next day for home. Most wondered why they didn't hire a guide on the first day instead of the last. I've wondered that also. Many anglers enjoy the challenge of new water, and if you have lots of time, it's a lot of fun. On the Missouri, a good guide will show you more in one day than you'll likely learn in a week on your own. The river changes and, unless you are on it most days, you won't be able to keep up with those changes.

Montana has outfitters, guides, booking agents, and shops that can fill your guided services needs. It's confusing to most people who don't work in the industry, but think of it this way—the outfitter is like the owner of an airline; he hires pilots (guides) to take you where you want to go. Booking agents and shops are like travel agencies who are able to place you, based on what you tell them you want. Most outfitters also guide and, if you like a particular one, will likely do their best to line you up with that person.

Many Montana guides are independent and work for several different outfitters. They use their own boats and gear. Law bars them from advertising their services, except in association with outfitters. Any guided trips done in the state must have an outfitter's endorsement, and be logged and reported to the Board of Outfitters.

The best guides get their dance cards filled early, especially in peak season. If you had a great time with a particular guide, bet that someone else did also. For July, which is peak dry fly season on the Missouri, many of the river's best guides are completely booked six to ten months in advance. You may drive into town and get a good guide during this time, but your chances are diminished if you wait that late.

What constitutes a good guide is probably at least somewhat subjective and dependent on your wants and style. You will find that some guides are very laid back while others are very intense. Some are patient instructors and some are not geared that way. The solution is to be specific when you ask for a guide. If you want lots of instruction, or if you are new to fly fishing, be candid about your abilities when talking to the shop or outfitter. The less you embellish (or downplay) your skills, the better match you will be given.

Before you get into the boat, remember to let the guide know what you are realistically expecting out of the day. If you would like to use the boat to move from one wading spot to another, you'll have to communicate that to him. Telling him only at the end of the day that you don't like fishing out of a drift boat won't help much. Most guides will try to accommodate your wants. If you only like to fish dry flies and the conditions are not suitable because of wind or lack of hatches, you may have to

Early season midge and Baetis *hatches draw anglers out of the house and onto the water.*

nymph, throw streamers, or wait patiently until the opportunity arises. Let him know your preference. Many of my clients prefer the top water action. I often rig up a dry fly rod and a nymph rod and if there are heads up and active eating on top, we fish top water. If there is no surface activity, you'll have to decide what to do until or if it happens.

Studded boots are great on slippery rivers but they are not well-suited to standing in a drift boat. They damage the boat and can be slippery on hard boat decks. The Missouri is not a tough river to wade fish. Without the slimy algae of a lot of trout streams, felt boots are enough here. If all you have are studded boots, make certain to tell the guide before you get in his boat.

Most guides on the Missouri bring water and soft drinks as well as lunch. They also supply the flies. Many of these flies are of their own design and cannot be bought. Consider how many flies of his you break off during the course of the day when it comes time to tip him. Most flies retail for around $2.

Most importantly, look at him as a consultant you've hired to assist you. Let him know your goals and then listen to what he has to say. If he's not going in the same direction that you want to go, let him know.

Most outfitters that work the Missouri have a web site. For a complete list of licensed outfitters go to Fishing Outfitters Association of Montana (FOAM) at www.foam-montana.org. If searching the web isn't your style, you can contact FOAM at (406) 763-5436.

Afterword

Fly fishing has become very popular in the last decade or so. Its elegance and grace have attracted the attention of many through movies and books. Like many sports it cannot ever really be mastered and it's that challenge that keeps it fresh and exciting. It's a chance to immerse yourself into nature, and standing in a good trout stream testing your skills is a great way to give yourself a break from the sometimes-chaotic world we live in. This very simple and quiet sport can transform you by making your world one of simple pleasures. It's a world without computers and fax machines, one without complexity. My hope is that you take the opportunity to experience this unique form of relaxation. I also hope that it changes your life forever, as it has mine.

The Missouri River is one of the very best trout streams I've ever had the privilege of dipping my felts into. It's *the* most consistent river as far as big strong fish.

As I look out my window at the snow-covered pines and hear the north wind whistling in the chimney of my wood stove, I know the Missouri is waiting for me in her slumber, calling me like a Siren calls the mariners to her. In a few months the *Baetis* will start popping and the creak of the oars on my boat will welcome me back after months of being covered and stored. Sure, I'll be out there this winter braving the cold feet and frozen rod guides. I'll feel the sun in my face and the bite of the wind against my skin. I'll watch for that window when the Midges excite the trout to the surface to feed and I might even hook up a few of

them. But mostly I'll go to the river to say hello to my old friend. The Missouri has been my friend for years, and my hope is that you will grow to befriend her also.

Trapper Badovinac